A Course in Tranquility

Ryan Kurczak

Copyright © 2010 Ryan Kurczak
All rights reserved.
ISBN-10: 1477678786
ISBN-13: 978-1477678787

DEDICATION

To Melissa and
Divine Providence.

CONTENTS

	Acknowledgments	i
1	Happiness for No Reason	1
2	Love and Relationships	23
3	Health	42
4	Vision and Purpose	54
5	Grace and Spiritual Practice	72
6	Absolving Your Past	90
7	Reality vs. Your Story	111
8	Practicing Your Faith	132
9	Forgiveness	153
10	Knowing the Truth of Unity Consciousness	175
11	Practices for Moving Fully as Your Self	188
12	What to Do When You Are Not Tranquil	204
13	Awareness Throughout the Day	217
14	Beyond the Cosmic Weather Patterns	237
	About the Author	256

ACKNOWLEDGMENTS

Thanks to all the clients and students, too numerous to mention, who shared so much of their lives, failures and successes, allowing the realization of how important it was to illustrate the techniques and philosophy outlined in these pages. You know who you are, and I acknowledge your support and presence.

And to all the teachers, authors and role models who helped clarify and distill the importance of purposeful living, meditation, and direct inquiry into life's most pressing question.

CHAPTER 1

HAPPINESS FOR NO REASON

"Learn to live a natural and spontaneous life, contentedly." According to the sage Vasistha, that is the point of all our striving. It is to this end, that we will direct our efforts through the practices and philosophy outlined in this book, that you may know the power of real tranquility.

By clearing away our false notions of reality and false ideas about who and what we really are, we will learn to exist in a natural state of peace. By challenging our preconceptions of what it means to be fully human and Self-realized, we will learn that it is as easy or as hard as we make it.

To be human is to have a body, personality, history, and a life story. To be Self-realized is to know, through direct experience, that we are immortal, eternal beings, only temporarily relating to the human condition. Self-realization is direct, conscious and unwavering realization of what modern scientists and mystics of all ages have known to be true: **that we are one with all life, that there is no separation between us and anything else, and that we can know it and be it without a doubt.**

There is no end to this thing called life, and we, our individual personalities, are unique and necessary expressions of it. It is by learning to function between two worlds, the limited world of the personality, and the infinite world which is the source of our very existence, that we learn to joyfully ride the rising and falling waves of divine creation.

When we can live from an expanded point of view, in full knowledge of our essence of being, we know what we are and what we are not, and are then free to move gracefully and dispassionately in, through and as the infinite consciousness. We are infinite consciousness expressing as individualized human beings.

Identification with the mind, our collection of thoughts, beliefs, and conditioning, is the root of the weed that prevents our natural spontaneity and peace. It is also the vessel that maintains our false sense of self, so that we are confined to act only within a certain set of parameters. We become so invested in this false sense of self that we defend it to the detriment of our quality of life. Stray too far outside the boundaries of who you think you are or what you think your life should be like, and prepare for the waves of anxiety, confusion and fear that will wash over you. All the terror is a mind-produced phenomena generated by our inability to accept our capacity to act as a limitless manifestation of unbounded possibilities.

Once we let go of the mind and let it function in its natural role, as a servant to our consciousness--calculator and recorder of data--we are free to turn our attention to more important matters, such as living.

Consider the quote from Alan Watts, "No work of love will flourish out of guilt, fear, or hollowness of heart, just as no valid plans for the future can be made by those who have no capacity for living now." Living now is an inside job. No matter how hard you try, there will never be any fulfillment from the external world. No situation, person, experience, place, or thing will ever fully satisfy you. There is no satisfaction in the future, and despite what you may falsely remember, there was never any satisfaction in the past. If you were ever truly satisfied, **it is because you chose to be**. You may have attached a reason to it, but that reason was just an after-thought, albeit a very subtle one.

The past and future are external creations, projections and recordings of past perceptions in the mind. A very efficient and quick way to restore the mind to its natural function is to stop waiting for the next moment. No doubt you have already experienced the fact that it is easier said than done. When you work, live, love and play without waiting for the next moment, everything you are and encounter flourishes.

The way to success in this endeavor returns us to our very Self, not the mind-imagined self, but our true eternal nature, the witnessing presence. When you find your self waiting for the next moment, admit it. Then ask yourself, "What is waiting for this next moment?" Of course the answer is "I am." We then take it a step further, "What am I?" Ask that question enough and sit quietly receptive and open to the answer, and you will move into a state of tranquility like you could never have imagined possible.

To develop the skill of receptivity to the answer, meditation is invaluable, and we will review that practice at the end of this chapter. It is impossible to really 'hear' the answer or experience the truth of what you are if we have not learned to turn down the static in our consciousness, and that is the point of meditation. For now, let us continue focusing on the living present.

In our efforts to stop waiting for the next moment, we can learn to experience our consciousness directly. We wait for the next moment because we are not comfortable where we are for one reason or another. We are uncomfortable because we do not remember what we truly are, and are avoiding reality. Finding reasons for our discomfort will only strengthen the identification with the mind, that very thing we are trying to uproot.

The best way to stop waiting for the next moment is to simply accept what consciousness is experiencing through your personality at this moment. If it is an uncomfortable feeling of dis-ease, just feel it. Do not continue to fool your self that something external in the future will change this feeling of dis-ease. Also, do not look to the past for the reason that you feel the way you do.

You can always find a reason to feel bad, just as you can always imagine a reason to feel good. It just depends on which habit you have strengthened most, feeling bad, or feeling great! The power in this practice is not finding or imagining reasons for your current state of consciousness, it is DECIDING to be different now FOR NO REASON. When you decide to be a certain way for no reason, then no reason can influence you to be a way you do not want to be. The mind feeds on reasons. You grow into tranquility by being free of reasons.

To avoid frustration, it is good to accurately judge your potential in this practice. If this is a new concept for you, your abilities to make these changes will, of course, be weak. Just as with all exercises, you start where you can and hold the intention of where you want to be until you get there. Then you become strong. Your mind may be strong and your tendency towards tranquility may be weak. Just admit it, if it is true. This state of affairs has occurred because you, like many people, have given more attention to the mind, rather than to a state of tranquility.

We are now undertaking the task of reversing that tendency. You will succeed so long as you never quit. This is exactly how all the other saints and sages of the world have become what they have become. They persevered.

Well-intentioned people may say that saints and sages are created through grace. Grace is involved, but not in the way you might imagine. As written in the bible, "God helps those who help themselves." Grace, like fate, is the accumulation of your present efforts to a desired end. So yes, God does help those who help themselves. No unit of consciousness has ever experienced sainthood without intention or practice.

What is a saint or a sage? A saint is a person who is completely and totally knowledgeable and identified with the Self. To say that a sage is the eternal Self is not entirely correct.

Otherwise we would all be saints. A realized holy person can be appropriate in any circumstance. When it is time to meditate, she can withdraw her attention into complete and total pure consciousness. When it is time to interact with a neighbor, or a family member, or to take any normal action in the world, she can do her best without attachment to the results of her actions.

Remember, the label saint or sage is just a role some people play. One can be Self and God-realized playing any role.

Saints do not have to act pious, or have any outward display of divinity. Saints that display fantastic powers do so for a reason. Their mission in the world may involve being spectacular in some way, but this is not a requirement. There are many people who can display fantastic feats and have interesting psychic abilities, but they have no idea about who or what they are, and so, still function out of an illusional sense of self, rather than a surrendered and appropriate expression of the infinite consciousness. Fantastic "spiritual powers" manifest spontaneously without premeditation through a saint. I mention this point, because it is not helpful to define your progress through any special abilities or perceptions. Our only point of measure should be the amount of tranquility and wisdom that comes as we mature into our intention to wake up fully.

Also remember, when involved in the world of form, emotions are common to everyone. Realized people feel emotions as well as everyone else. They can also choose to express or not express certain emotions, good or bad. They are free, so they are free to do what is appropriate. The difference between a realized person and others, is that the realized person is not attached to emotional states or expressions. They are free to be fully human and fully divine simultaneously, and all that implies. When you directly experience that you are a realized sage, you too will have that same latitude.

According to sage Patanjali, "Yoga is the cessation of fluctuations in the field of consciousness. When the fluctuations cease, the seer abides in its own nature. At other times there is conformity to definitions." Yoga in this context refers to a complete realization of the unity of consciousness. The result is perfect peace and tranquility. With the ending of fluctuations (or the need to think and label), Self-realization shines forth of its own accord. We are completely fulfilled. When focused on the "changes" or "differences" in consciousness, we are bound again to live in delusion and thereby forget our tranquility.

The idea of changes or fluctuations in consciousness is just that, an idea. To clarify, note the words of Vasistha, "Even as the mirage appears to be a very real river of water, this creation appears to be entirely real. And as long as one clings to the notion of the reality of "you" and "I", there is no liberation." The notions of "you" and "I" are labels created by the mind. We are inseparable. When we dream, who are the characters in the dream? Are they not a manifestation of the same one thing? The same is true for our waking dream. To continue to enforce labels, rather than simply acting appropriately and knowing this whole experience is just one thing, we continue our existence in bondage. Begin to accept, that this, your experiences, is all you.

You may not have the power to fully realize that, or to even understand what this will mean once you fully grasp it. But if you are going to entertain a notion, "This is all me" is a good one to hold.

Vasistha continues, "Not by merely and verbally denying such a notion of existence is it obliterated: on the contrary, such denial itself becomes a further distraction." To deny the existence of a problem simply enforces it. To say, "I'm working hard to gain liberation and perfect peace," generates the notion, that you do not have liberation or peace. You are affirming that which you do not want to experience without your knowing. **You are liberation and peace.** To say, "I am making my self well through this practice, because there was something fundamentally wrong with me before," has the same effect. **There is nothing wrong with you.** You have just been affirming your current state through your actions, thoughts and words. Now it is time to affirm that which you do want to experience.

This brings us to the secret key many spiritual teachers leave out. Practice is done for the joy of doing the practice, not for a result. If you like to meditate, that is excellent! Meditate because you like it. If you like to pray for peace, that's good, do it for its own sake. If you enjoy reading spiritual or philosophical literature, do so, not because it will make you better or because it is good for you, but because that is what consciousness enjoys doing through you. Play music, dance, and cook, serve the homeless or work hard at your job. If you need a reason, do it because that is what you, the Self, enjoys doing through you as an individualized unit of its own wholeness. The real eternal you, is not going to get any better. Not even with age.

Now there may be experiences you would like to have which involve doing things you do not particularly enjoy. In our current cultural atmosphere, sitting to meditate for an hour a day, being benevolently truthful, eating a non-fad nutrition rich diet, being content for no reason, working to have adequate resources to accomplish goals and even regular exercise—all actions conducive to the practice of experiencing liberation of consciousness—a lot of people do not like to do. This again comes down to choice and how badly you would like to experience the life you want. If you do not want to harness your will to overcome attachments to your current experience, and are not willing to master your state of consciousness to move beyond debilitating aversions, at least be honest with your self about it. There is no need to feel guilt about your choice. Either you do or you don't. It's up to you. Being peacefully self honest about it, is a good first step. Keep it up for long enough, and you may find that you eventually start moving in the direction of liberation and realization effortlessly.

Remember, you are the Self. Nothing can make you the Self, or take you away from the Self. It is you. Now that we have that cleared up, the important question arises, as stated so well by one spiritual teacher, "How do you want to be living your immortal life?" This is what I would like you to think about as we move through this book.

If you already have a clear idea, write it down. Hold that intention as we proceed. If you do not yet know, hold the intention *that you do know* how you want to live your immortal life. Affirm it with conviction daily. When you feel lost or confused do not affirm the feeling of doubt. Chase it away however you can, and bring back up the feeling of what it would be like to be completely and totally knowledgeable. You do not have to have the information in your mind immediately.

Remember, there is more to you than the mind. Through affirmation and adopting the feeling state, you are accessing the information. Be patient as the rest of your being, the infinite consciousness, gathers the opportunities to reveal it to you.

With every breath and movement, feel as though you are, at this very moment, living a natural and spontaneous life, contentedly. In all circumstances, whether you judge the circumstance to be perfect or imperfect, good or bad, pleasant or unpleasant, accept that this is your natural and spontaneous life; the accumulation of all your present choices, thoughts and words up to this point.

Be content to let the accumulated force exhaust itself. It has to one way or the other. To deny this is to deny reality, and that will not help. As the accumulated force loses its momentum, make the choices that are conducive to your ideal experience as an expression of the infinite consciousness.

Review this writing before sleep at night or during leisure time. Contemplate that which you do not understand, and put into action what you do understand. It will become clearer with repeated contact.

We learn best by doing, and the following exercises will serve to provide a foundation for understanding this material.

Meditation helps to organize and balance our mind and nervous system. A clear head and a healthy inner environment makes it possible to have the energy and motivation to understand clearer states of consciousness and to live from those states. Organizing your life will serve to keep you from wasting time and encourage a purposeful interaction with the people and world around you. The more time and energy you have for inner work, the quicker you will wake up, spiritually speaking.

Exercise #1

Deepen a Regular Meditation Practice

First sit in a comfortable position with your back straight. Close your eyes and look slightly upward gazing into the darkness of your eyelids. Upward gazing will keep you alert and awake. Take a few deep breaths, and feel the air come in and leave your body. With each exhalation let your worries or concerns fall away. As you settle into a relaxed attentive state set your intention to experience the essence of divinity within and without you. This can be done with a prayer if you are inclined. Now, return your attention to your breath.

For the next fifteen minutes just breath, and be aware of breathing. Should thoughts arise, let them pass. Remember to give yourself fully to the practice. Become absorbed in the breath, prayer or stillness. This is the time for inner rejuvenation. You have all day to attend to other matters. After any form of distraction, gently return your attention to your breathing. When you are ready, drop the breath from your attention. Rest within the stillness that has been allowed to emerge from this simple practice.

After a few weeks gaining proficiency in the above routine, utilizing the following schedule can deepen the practice. Twice a day sit for thirty to forty-five minutes. Set aside the same time every day. Sit where you will not be disturbed. Take a few deep breaths and get comfortable with your back straight. Close your eyes and direct your attention within. Again, looking slightly upward to stay alert and affirm your innate divine nature.

Recite a memorized prayer, or pray spontaneously silently to allow the connection with the divine to become more real. Now, use a two word phrase to direct your attention. This can be as simple as "Peace, love" or any other word that positively attracts your attention. With your breathing recite your word phrase. On the inhale, listen to the first word inside your head. On the exhale, listen to the second word. Let it fill your entire awareness. Give all of your attention to it.

Should thoughts or distractions arise, gently bring your attention back to your word phrase and breathing. Practice feeling the word phrase resonating in your awareness for the next ten to fifteen minutes. This will calm the mind and allow the body to relax deeply. Now rest in this relaxed, yet alert peaceful state. Remain calm and poised for as long as possible.

Once internal or external distractions begin to make themselves known, start over again. Continue practicing in this way until you have reached your prescribed time. Finish with a silent prayer, and acknowledge the divine peace you experienced, and let it fill your day.

After resting for a while in the pure state of awareness you may conclude and go about your day, or remain a little longer engaging in constructive problem solving. It is after the practice that we can most appropriately address any issues in our lives that need it. When our awareness is not clouded by overactive thoughts or emotions we are more easily able to understand why things are the way they are. With this understanding proper action can be taken to change. This practice creates the structure in life for the unfoldment of Self-realization and spiritual knowledge. Without this understanding we wander pointlessly into suffering.

Each day we meditate or pray to realize our spiritual purpose and how it transposes into our physical life, we lay a few more bricks into the structure. With patience and consistency we will eventually wake up to find that the last brick was set yesterday morning, and from there all we need do is let life happen spontaneously and constructively.

Exercise #2

Stop Waiting for the Next Moment

Whatever you are doing in your day, do it fully. Focus on the action. Just do the action. There is no need to think about it, unless thinking is the action. Once you are done with one action, move on to the next. It is helpful to make a list the night before of what you intend to accomplish the next day. Here is an example list:

1. Meditate.

2. Shower.

3. Go to work. (You could also make a list of what you will do while at work.)

4. Exercise for 45 minutes.

5. Pay due bills

6. Practice my musical instrument.

7. Clean the kitchen after dinner

8. Watch favorite show.

9. Check the mail.

10. Read "Yoga Sutras."

11. Meditate.

12. Make 'to do' list for tomorrow.

Now you do not have to think about your day. You know what you are going to do. You can now focus on one thing at a time. Mark out each action as they are completed. This will also help you feel a sense of accomplishment as your day progresses.

There may be points through out the day when you are unhappy or uncomfortable with the present circumstance. That's natural until you learn to be content all the time. What is the best way to deal with moments like that?

First, admit that you feel the way you do. Then if you find your self thinking that something in the future would change it, stop. More than likely, you would just feel better temporarily, and then once that is cleared up, something else would come up and you would think that there must be something else. It's an endless cycle. So just stop it now. Next, you will probably look for something or someone in the past to blame your unpleasant state on. Stop that too. Don't blame, just feel what you feel. It will quit eventually.

Stay in reality, and the relative reality may be that you feel uncomfortable. Leave the past and future alone. Does this idea make sense? No, of course not. Your mind would like it to though, wouldn't it? Stay vigilant and continue the practice. You will eventually have the direct experience, that how you feel is not dependant on the past or the future, and that you can always find a reason to feel how you do. Forget about reasons. Focus on choice.

Choose what you want to feel and feel it. Don't wait for the next moment.

Be with what is, and once you are comfortable with that, then choose what is. You are learning to develop control over your states of consciousness, a key skill for any Self-realized person.

CHAPTER 2

LOVE AND RELATIONSHIPS

Swami Sri Yukteswar, a spiritual teacher from India, once said, "Ordinary love is selfish, darkly rooted in desires and satisfactions. Divine love is without condition, without boundary, without change. The flux of the human heart is gone forever at the transfixing touch of pure love."

How many of us can love like that? How many want to? Only a handful.

To love in this way requires a strong and decisive act of will to ignore the culturally ingrained ideas and adolescent attitudes most of us have about what love is meant to be like.

To love in this way requires total immersion in our divine presence that is tranquil in all circumstances, and sees everyone equally as a unique expression of the one infinite consciousness.

Think of all the stories of romance, of heroes overcoming great odds to be with the beloved, of how a person's life was perfected the moment they found that special someone. Those are stories and fantasy, and we want to be in reality as much as possible, right? Of course we do. Only there will we find perfect peace and real love.

Get it out of your head that there is a special someone, or that your life would be different if only your family or friends would change, or that things would be so much better if your lover finally became the person you always expected him or her to be.

In my astrological practice I am often asked about relationships. When will it get better? Should I leave my husband? Is there someone better out there for me? Why do my friends always drag me down? How can I ever forgive her for cheating on me? It goes on. Remember that your astrological chart (and we all have one) reflects your individual karma.

Unless you have exhausted a karma, if you leave or change a relationship, without changing you, that pattern will continue to express in whatever new relationships you find.

To exhaust your relationship karma a decision is made. Decide that you have had enough of the relationship experiences you have been attracting. Really mean it! No longer will you put your happiness in the hands of 'other' people, by having expectations of what they should be like, and then being disappointed when they simply act as they are. To exhaust your karma in relationships first requires that you take the time to pay attention to how people really are, to love and bless them in all their actions, and then to intentionally decide if you really want to be a part of all that a relationship with that person entails.

Exercise #1

Step 1 – When going into an interaction with anyone, remember that most people are on autopilot 95% of the time. Their actions are based on conditioning, how they've been raised, how they choose to see the world, and their motives in life, most of which they are not even aware.

Step 2 – Practice bringing conscious awareness into your relationships, specifically the ones you would like to change. To do this, remember your past encounters with the person you are about to interact with. How did they make you feel? Bad? Guilty? Shameful? Worthless? Stupid? Anxious? Fearful? What did they do or say to make you feel that way? What language did they use? How did they catch you off guard? What did they talk about? Etc.

Pay attention to their patterns of interaction. Remember those patterns before you go into the interaction, either in person or on the phone. Then watch and wait for those patterns to repeat, and observe how they make you feel the way you always do, like clockwork, when you are interacting with this person.

Step 3 – Don't judge these people. You do it too! The point of all this is to bring you in line with reality, so you can see, that the way people act towards you is nothing personal. They are on autopilot, and you happen to be receptive to their programming.

Your karma matches up. It's as much your fault as it is theirs.

Step 4 – Don't try to change them. You will only frustrate yourself. Admit the truth of how they affect you and love them. Decide if you really want to continue playing this game with them. If so, fine. If not, don't engage the program. It's up to you!

The more skillful you become with this exercise, the more comical it will become. You will no longer be triggered, and it becomes a game. "How are they going to try and trigger me this time," you will ask. Most of the time you will catch it, before it happens, before they do their usual spiel that will make you feel untranquil. As you continue the relationship they will unconsciously learn that they no longer have an effect on you. Then you will relax, thinking you have it mastered, and BAM!, somehow they will find another way to ruffle you, to your surprise.

You won't take it so personally, unless it's terribly cruel, and you will chuckle to yourself. They got me that time!

But this is not about wasting your time playing games with people. It is about seeing the truth of the quality of the relationship. It is about inspiring you to see "realistically" where you are in life in regards to relationships. This creates the ground work, the foundation, for you to begin the process of change, of attracting what you do want out of your interactions with people.

In a book called, "The Cosmic Power Within" by Dr. Joseph Murphy, he speaks of tapping into our Cosmic Power, our divine essence, to create the life we want. The exercise below, based on Dr. Murphy's work, if used persistently, will give the results you would like to see. The cosmic power within is based on your ability to 'see' and 'feel' a different result, and then to allow the infinite consciousness (the totality of your being) to bring the opportunities into your life to allow that different state to express.

Remember, this is not about deserving, it is simply about deciding. If you have "deserving" issues, it is only because you have decided to have an excuse not to live freely in this world, or to access the creative power of your spirit. You are strong! You are wonderful! You are able to generate any life experience you want with enough Self-effort. You may have just been listening to the wrong people. Tune in to those who support this knowledge, and you will be supported.

Exercise #2

Step 1 – Choose a relationship you would like to see improved in some way. Take out a sheet of paper and write down specifically the improvement you'd like to see and why you'd like to see it. There needs to be a tangible reason to empower this process. This reason is of your own choosing. Don't base it on society or what others tell you is a good reason. You are learning to become Self-directed.

Step 2 – Imagine how it would feel if that relationship were already perfect. What kinds of emotions would you have around this person? What would the quality of your interactions be like? Write down your ideal feeling state. Put your piece of paper somewhere safe, for you to review or edit as necessary.

Step 3 – Once or twice a day, spend five minutes feeling the state you decided on in step 2. Even if it is hard, or you have a hard time getting in touch with feelings, do it anyway. It will be good practice.

Step 4 – Since this will have to do with a particular relationship, you need to associate those feelings with the relationship. Let's take a spousal relationship for example. When you are feeling that state, say to your self, "I feel [Insert Emotional State] when I am around my spouse." And then do what ever it takes to make yourself feel this deeply. Do not see your spouse specifically. Think of 'wife' or 'husband' or 'partner' almost like a general term or an archetype.

Now why are we using the archetype for spouse? Because we are not black magicians and we are not trying to manipulate a specific person. What we are doing is changing the "spouse" pattern within us. Once that pattern changes, the external world will follow. Either you will see that the spouse 'out there' was that way all along, or she will feel inspired to change, or she will like who she is, and move on to someone who appreciates her particular patterns of being. Either way, you will get what you want.

Step 5 – Repeat this process every day, until you have sculpted your inner reality as perfectly as you like. Also, note, you are only doing this for five minutes once or twice a day.

Once it is done for the day, stop. Quit thinking about it. Don't dwell. Just move on with your day. There is no need to get your conscious mind obsessed with this practice.

This process can be applied to spouses, friends, brothers, sisters, coworkers, bosses, mothers, fathers, etc.

Now back to divine love...

When you look back on your life I am sure it is filled with a mixture of pleasant and unpleasant memories. There were times when you felt great love, anger, peace, hatred, laughter, resentment, joy and grief. There were times when people treated you in ways that exceeded your expectations and other times when you wished people treated you better. You may have often wondered at why people did what they did, what their motivation was to be so kind or so despicable.

As I was meditating a few years back a flood of memories pushed up from my subconscious. I remembered all kinds of interactions with people and the corresponding feelings from those moments past. A whirl of emotions ran through me. After they passed a realization dawned. Every experience I have had, no matter if I labeled it good or bad, was an act of love.

How can this be?! You might ask your self. I understand that all the good things I've experienced are an act of love, but how can the bad be love too? If you take the time to observe the interactions you have with people you might notice one familiar component. Almost everyone you interact with is gaining your attention or giving you attention.

How they do that is an individual preference based on how they were raised, taught to behave, and a little of their own experimentation in the process. Maybe they buy you flowers, clean the house before you get home, hit you, call you names, flatter you, give you a massage, cook you dinner, or undermine your confidence. Some are easier to digest, and some are perverted actions of the initial impulse. Many people are unconscious and do the nice things out of compulsion or fear because they don't want to lose you. Others act in menacing ways because they don't know any better. The point is, in any interaction there is an exchange of attention. It is attention that is love.

Many years ago I discovered that no matter what healing protocol I chose from, the force that empowered all healing was attention. The clearer my attention, the less of an agenda I had to disrupt my attention, the more authentic was the healing experience. The same holds true in all human interactions. The clearer and less distracted your attention is on the person in which you are interacting, the greater the love that is generated.

When you decide to give someone attention with conditions, you are giving conditional love, which may be helpful when certain conditions are met. You say, "I will give you love when you stop nagging me, or when you learn to appreciate how I'm different than you!" Then you wait for the love to be returned and they do the same, providing the same conditions. Really, if you are nagging a person to stop nagging you so that you can give them love, its the same thing.

They nag you because they want you to be different, because their mind impels them to think your life would be better if you were different. That's love. Why? Because the motivation behind it is for your highest and best (as they see it). You hope they will be different because you really would like to spend some "quality time" (by your standards) with them without all the stress. That's love too.

Now back to my point. It may not be that people will give you love the way you want it, but they will give you love the way they know how. It may not be pleasant, but it is still love nonetheless. In unpleasant situations you don't always have to accept the conditional love you are being given. You can remove yourself from the situation, and that is sometimes necessary and beneficial. However, if you decide to love without condition, which also means without expectations, you may catch a glimpse of real love at work within your relationships.

By expectations I mean that you do not expect the people in your life to be any different than they have proven to be in the past. When you can love them as they are, you in turn will set the example to be loved as you are. You will bring into the relationship a dynamic they have never experienced before: peace, acceptance, and no standards (unspoken or not) to live up to.

All of this begins with you and no one else. It is your responsibility, whether you want it or not. When you claim it for your self, you will find the strength of love in your life that you have been looking for all this time.

Love and Tranquility – The Holy Life

"The Virtue of Love, the Heart's natural love, is the principal requisite to attain a holy life. When this love, the heavenly gift of Nature, appears in the heart, it removes all causes of excitation from the system and cools it down to a perfectly normal state; and, invigorating the vital powers, expels all foreign matters- the germs of diseases-by natural ways (perspiration and so forth). It thereby makes man perfectly healthy in body and mind, and enables him to understand properly the guidance of Nature.

"When this love becomes developed in man it makes him able to understand the real position of his own Self as well as of others surrounding him." –Sri Yukteswar

Being in a state of love, bliss and ease, was not easy for me. Students that attend my classes are often amazed to hear that during the first part of my life, I was irritable, pessimistic, often unpleasant, unhappy, angry, and had a cruel streak. Smiling genuinely and being pleasant was a foreign state for me to experience. Why? Because I didn't have much practice in existing in a state of love and peace. Much of how I interacted with the world was either out of fear or domination.

It took me a number of years to learn to feel love and be in a state of love. Meditation made it much easier, because it allowed me to see the patterns and choices I had made that contributed to this state of affairs. By an act of will and conscious effort I had to make my self feel love and be love. This was an inward process, and not one dependant on others recognizing it.

I had no reason to make this choice. Being trapped in the mind, and my little sense of self that was created out of unconscious desires and cravings, it was insane to even think it was safe to love and be loved. It made no sense. I did it anyway, because an urge within me indicated that it was possible to be different, and that if I could be different, reality would change accordingly.

Slowly, as the years rolled by, my persona changed. I learned to be at ease. For the most part, I learned not to sweat all the fearful ideas the normal human condition likes to entertain. I learned to trust in the goodness of the world, and the wholeness of life. The more I surrendered into the process, the easier it became to smile from a place of real warmth. I learned that if I wanted to be in a state of love, I had to cut out relationships that were fear/domination based, and seek out relationships that were natural, supportive and positively challenging when necessary.

Twelve years after I graduated from high school and ten years into my practice of meditation and the techniques taught in these lessons, I met with a girl with whom I went to school. We hadn't seen each other in that time. As we sat having tea at a bookstore, halfway through the conversation, she asked if there was something wrong with me. She said, she had never seen me smile so much, and that I appeared totally different than the angst-ridden person she had known previously. I didn't really notice how major the changes were in myself until she pointed it out.

Sometimes changes can occur and we are not aware of it, because we are always with our selves. It is just like aging. One day you look in the mirror after seeing a picture of your self twenty years earlier and you notice the difference. Since you see your self in the mirror every day, you don't notice how age has progressed until you have a point of reference to compare it to.

I'm telling you this, because I want you to take time with your self. Unless you have a spontaneous enlightenment experience, your changes will be gradual. If you are not used to feeling love or being love, it will take time. Be patient and let it unfold. Stay steady with the intention and it will occur.

Here is an exercise I use daily. It has contributed greatly to expanding my mind and consciousness to encourage the experience of personal, divine and cosmic love in my life.

Exercise #3

Step 1 – After your regular meditation practice, remember a time you felt completely content, when all was good and right in the world. Remember a time you felt fulfilled and in perfect love. You can use a past memory to bring up this state.

Step 2 – Imagine that you are feeling that state for no reason at all. That is just the current state of the Universe that you happen to be in. Intensify the feeling if you can. If you are not used to that feeling, practice will increase your skill.

Step 3 – With your eyes closed, imagine that feeling of love radiating beyond your body and through the universe to every person, place, animal, and thing in existence. Feel as though you are a beacon of light and this feeling is permeating all aspects of creation. Hold that feeling and imagination for as long as possible.

Step 4 – When you can no longer maintain this visualization/feeling, let it go. Just drop it. Say a prayer of thanks for the opportunity to be in love. Then go about your day.

Do this every day, and treat it like exercise. The radiance of your love is to be unconditional. Send it to all beings, whether you feel they are deserving or not. Do not try to change anyone or anything through this love. Just radiate it freely, as freely as the sun shines on all people without concern of their personality or deeds.

You may find you have a hard time doing this, or that you can only maintain this state for only a second. Remember, it is exercise. You will get stronger in love every day you do it. Soon you will be able to sit for five, ten, twenty minutes, or even an hour in a state of love. Then you will know real service to the world, and your life will change accordingly.

This simple exercise is not to be overlooked. I have meditated many times, contemplating, "What is the source of life?" "What is the meaning of all of this?" "What is the point?" Every single time, as my mind became silent and I was open to hear the answer, it was always this, "Love." I then knew through direct experience, that the words of Sri Yuktewswar, written earlier in this chapter, were absolutely correct.

CHAPTER 3

CONSIDERATIONS ON HEALTH

Vitality, strength, proper hormonal balance, an effective immune system, psychological and mental poise, good digestion, and proportional body mass all contribute to good health. They are also the *indicators* of good health. While a person can be spiritually awake and peaceful inside while lacking one or more of these characteristics, the happier we become, the easier it will be for us to manifest radiant health in all ways. Conversely, the more we direct our intention to manifesting these characteristics, our joyousness in life grows too.

To move towards tranquility, requires that we do what is necessary to provide the proper field for the seeds of tranquility to sprout. The area of health is not something to be lightly overlooked in this regard. When we have health, we are free to direct our attention to other areas of life, such as doing the divine work that we are here to manifest, which is where our real joy comes from anyway, believe it or not.

An unhealthy mind and body, is a distraction from the ultimate task at hand, and many people make the study of health, or their own fixation on health issues a vocation that perpetually gets in the way of serving and living in the highest way. This is why I say, we must give our attention to doing what we must to maintain our health, but we do need to avoid our fixation on health.

There are certain things we can do to ensure health. They are: exercise, plenty of rest, a nutrition-rich diet, sunshine, daily meditation to cleanse the mental field, and a positive and forward looking attitude. Be a possibility thinker, rather than someone who expects the worst. Surrounding your self with happy and successful people is also useful. If you are not happy or successful, you will have to learn that skill by experience to fit in with those folks who are happy and successful.

Many sages advise the company of "holy" people as a supreme source of positive growth. This is because you will become like those people you surround yourself with. What do you want to be like? Find those individuals and jump on the wagon! It won't take long and you will soon be a totally different person.

I have found that when I exercise, I always seem to find my self working out with the Ex-Air Force officer who likes to mountain bike like a professional, peddling straight up a mountain for 5 miles, or the intense aerobics instructor who likes to push her self to the limits. What effect does that have on me? I either learn to be like them or I doubt they would spend much time with me. I then become a more fit and healthy person.

When it comes to friendships and acquaintances, I make sure that those people I spend my time with are drama-free and creative in some way. They are also often very giving and in some form of service to the world. What influence does this have on me? I become that way too. I become a better person. I would rather be alone than to waste my time with problem-centered, small-minded, petty people. Wouldn't you? I hope so!

I gave the previous examples because earlier in my life I thought exercise was a waste of time. I also found myself cavorting with less than desirable individuals. The result was that I was unhealthy, and had a bad attitude about life. Now I realize that I feel a lot better about myself and the world when I maintain my current choices to be fit and part of an uplifting crowd of people.

Health and Wellness Rule #1

Be aware of those people, places, attitudes, and actions that get in the way of healthy happy living. Then do your best to avoid them.

Remember always that you are not taking action to strengthen your health only to prevent, or fight off potential disease. You are exercising, meditating, eating fresh whole foods, and surrounding yourself with positive people, because you are here to enjoy a life affirming existence! You are here to love being alive and feeling your own vitality, the spirit of the divine moving through you. You are here to give your gifts to the world joyfully! That is why you take action for perfect health.

Why do I bring this up? I've worked with many people in the past ten years in my healing practice. I've also spent a fair amount of time focusing on healing and strengthening my own body. I've seen what gets in the way of healing, and believe it or not, aside from the poor diet, lack of exercise, **it is the attitude behind the process that makes all the difference**.

Imagine a person exercising on a treadmill every day. The thoughts that go through the mind as this person slugs through another hour of heart pumping footwork, usually goes something like this, "My dad died of a heart attack. My doctor says I have high cholesterol. I don't want to die!" All the while, with each step, they are really affirming the fear they want to avoid.

Now imagine someone who is getting the most benefit out of their exercise routine and actually extending their life. They wake up in the morning and say, "I can't wait to get to the gym! It feels so great to get my blood pumping! I love feeling alive. I love being able to walk up steep mountain trails and the stairs at my work with out getting winded! This body is great and allows me to live and do so much!"

That is quite a different attitude. You see, one person is affirming life and the fact that a healthy body allows her to live all the more fully. The other is acting out of fear and strengthening the negative energy she is trying to avoid.

Health and Wellness Rule #2

If you are going to exercise, love it because it makes you stronger, and better able to live your life freely. Really bring up a sense of joy with each activity you undertake that strengthens your body.

The same goes for food. Think of all the people you know who avoid certain foods like the plague or claim they are allergic to everything. There is a biologic reason for this, for most people. However, interestingly enough, I have paid close attention to the attitudes of people with food and digestion problems, and they are very similar. They do not feel safe in the world. Also, they usually (unconsciously of course) either like the attention they get by needing a special diet, or they are simply putting their problems onto food, to avoid dealing with the real issues behind their disturbance.

Imagine the following. Every time person A eats, he thinks, "Is there something bad for me in this food? Is this going to make me sick? Am I too sensitive to this? Is it organic? Has it been fried with meat products?!" Every time person B eats, she thinks, "I love how healthy this fresh fruit makes me. I love the strength these whole grains and this organic cheese gives my body. I love giving my body this fresh life force through my food so I can live my best life!" Which one of those folks do you imagine is going to have the healthier body, as well as, be able to eat just about whatever they want?

Health and Wellness Rule #3

Eat whole foods. With each bite, feel fresh life and divine energy entering your body. Think positively about the food you eat.

Believe it or not, your feelings about those things you do to support your health make a HUGE difference as to whether or not they really support your health. I've seen plenty of health fanatics who take tons of supplements and go to all the right experts, still have serious health problems. Why? Because they make a big deal about health, and don't make a big deal about living. This is about LIFE, remember. You are here to live, not to try and line up every possibility perfectly. Do your best, and let the divine take care of the rest, and most of all feel good about what you do for yourself and others. Otherwise, what's the use in doing it?

I'm not implying it's easy if you are used to thinking negatively, but the only person that can change that is you. You got yourself into that place to begin with. Only you can get your self out. The sooner you accept that, the better!

Health and Wellness Rule #4

Don't make health your primary focus in life, otherwise that is what it will become. Make living and contributing to the world your focus. Do what you know is good for your health, and then let it go, and live!

Even people who do their best, think positively and genuinely enjoy living have health issues to deal with from time to time. It's not a sign of failure, just part of the process of being alive.

There are so many theories, ideas, teachers, healers, and health systems that it can be hard to know which one to utilize. Some even contradict each other, which makes matters worse. So how do you know where to get good information?

You are a unique mind/body/spirit unit. What works for you might not work for your neighbor. Your personality may respond better to certain treatments. Some people need allopathic medical treatments to get well, while others may heal beautifully by taking Chinese herbs for six months. Some people have a biologic or genetic issue causing their lack of health, while others, demonstrating the same symptoms, may be suffering from a psychic or psychological disturbance. There is no ultimate right way to heal. There is only your way.

It is good to research various systems to find the one that resonates with you. However, as is recommended on the spiritual path, it is not advised to mix practices frivolously. If you find a system that works, stick with it. Some things take time and persistence, and if you have something that works that feels right, and is getting results, there is no need to be impatient.

Health and Wellness Rule #5

Healing takes commitment. Find a system that works for you and stick with it. To think that there is a better one out there, is the 'Grass is Always Greener' syndrome. Health is a way of life, whether Ayurvedic, Traditional Chinese Medicine, Allopathic, etc.

A health professional should inspire you to wellness, not shock you with fear, or generate anxiety, worry or depression of any kind. They will be truthful, but not fatal. A health professional with a trust in the divine power, and a peaceful countenance is most beneficial. They can be allopathic doctors, or acupuncturists. Admittedly rare, a health care provider with heightened spiritual awareness is the best.

Again, second opinions are good, but if you find a wellness provider that you trust, has provided good service to you in the past, and is competent, it is best to maintain a consistent relationship rather than bouncing around from one person to the next.

As the years go by, the health care provider gets to know your health and disease tendencies and so can work with you specifically out of experience. You also benefit by getting to know how your health care provider works, and so trust develops. If there is no trust or rapport it is hard to develop a healing relationship.

Remember, health and wellness is a multifaceted path encompassing proper living, good information, supportive practitioners, positive attitude and trust in a higher power. Once we are in our right place in life, health and wellness need not be our main concern. By developing proper habits, we can let our health be, and focus on more important matters in life.

CHAPTER 4

VISION AND PURPOSE

We are each individualized expressions of consciousness. What does that mean? It means that we are a condensation of Infinity. Imagine that there is a field of being that has no boundary and no limitation. You can envision it like an immense ocean. Now, from time to time, that ocean becomes more dense. Consider a flat cloth sheet spread across a table. Now imagine pressing your finger on the sheet and twisting it, so that the sheet bunches up around your finger. The field bunches up into an "individual". The field becomes contracted and it experiences itself with attributes. It gains a sense of self, it feels that it is an individual. It gains a personality, an idea of history. It is then able to feel itself and begins to "think" that it is different than the space around it.

Assume, as the sage Vasistha would have you do, that this field takes shape, much like a block of gold can be shaped into a bracelet. The biggest problem we all have to face is the forgetfulness that although we are no longer identified with the formless field, we are still that field, just as the bracelet is really still gold. To feel separate from God or the Divine is just as absurd as the bracelet bemoaning that it has become a bracelet and lost its "goldness".

Yogananda said that, "the purpose of life is much different than what most people believe." He is correct. The purpose of life is to wake up to your immortal nature. It's to realize that, yes, you currently identify with a form, but that really you are the wholeness of life. I've heard my meditation teacher say before, that when you meditate, "feel as though you are in God." I followed this advice for a long time. Then one day, it occurred to me. 'Since we are not separate from God or the infinite, why not meditate as though we are the infinite!?' You then realize that you are what God is doing right now.

We are raised on stories of heroes saving the day and taught that we need to overcome odds and achieve glory, fame, money, a big house, the perfect family, etc. Our need for a purpose is extremely strong. However, the question I'd like to encourage you to ask your self is, "What needs a purpose?" Obviously you will say that "You do!" But that is not true. Remember, the real you is immortal, changeless, timeless, infinite. Yet something within encourages you that there must be a purpose to your life to be happy and successful. You can meditate on this, and I highly advise that, so that you get the direct experience of this knowledge.

I'm going to go ahead and give the actual answer to this question, "Who needs a purpose?" The mind needs a purpose. You are not the mind. Yet you have a mind, and it's not happy unless it's got something to think about. Hence, one thing that will keep it thinking for centuries is "What's my purpose?" Why is this the case? If you had a purpose, you would be acting on it and not wondering what it is. We'll discuss how to remedy the "I Need a Purpose" problem later in the chapter.

I'd like to encourage you to think about something to help bring this home. When you look to nature, do you wonder, "What's the purpose?" If so, why, do you wonder what the purpose of nature is?

Does nature wonder, "what's the purpose of my existence?" No. So why should you? Think about dancing. Is the purpose of dancing to get from point A to point B? Think about music. Is the purpose to get to the end of a song? You may have heard theories that all of this experience is God's play, or that life is a cosmic dance. So what's the purpose of playing and dancing? Simply, to do it.

Now, it is obvious that we, being individualized units of infinity, do have specific roles to play in this divine drama. If we want to think about it, think of it as though we are each individual cells of a larger organism. You are not different from the organism, because you came out of its substance, but you take shape to express certain aspects so that the organism may experience life.

Before we go into more detail about what you, as an individual "should" be doing with your life, please take some time to answer the following questions. Write as much as you want, but be sure to write at least three good sentences for each question. This will start the process of being able to really question your ideas about purpose, and bring some more clarity along the way.

So You Need a Purpose

1) In an ideal world, what would your purpose be?

2) Are you living in the world, acting in a way, or doing work that you do not enjoy or that you find meaningless?

3) Where do you think meaning comes from?

4) Why are you living like you are living now?

5) Who told you to live this way? Why did you listen?

6) Do you think fulfillment is going to come when you accomplish that one specific thing, meet that one specific person, or acquire a certain predetermined status?

7) What is wrong with right now?

8) When you are in your day, and you are doing your job, or interacting with certain people, are there particular moments that just are not right? Are you sure? How can you tell?

9) What makes you think that one moment is better than another?

10) What would it mean to you if you know, in your heart of hearts, your sense of meaning is really only dependant on your attitude and choice to imbue something with meaning and purpose?

Avoid Wasting Your Life Wondering

As we go along, we need to realize that one of the biggest blocks to experiencing real tranquility is thinking too much. As mentioned before, yes, we do need to be able to think. We need to be able to reason, to balance our check book, to make a plan of action, to assess the merit or demerit of a situation, but once these actions are completed, thinking does not need to continue.

As mentioned above, wondering what your purpose is, is one sure fire way to waste endless moments of time thinking and not being in a tranquil space. The real reason we think too much is to avoid making decisions. Why? Usually it's because we don't want to fail. We want to make sure we are making the right decision. We think that, if we only made that one perfect decision, everything would work out in a fairy tale ending, AND THEN we can relax and be tranquil.

This leads us back to the ideal of spiritual practice as daily living: to act in the world, while letting go of the fruits of our actions. Take some time to think about this. Can anyone, even the most talented expert in a field, completely control the outcomes of their actions? We can live perfectly skillfully, and yes this has merit. It keeps us out of a lot of trouble and gives us a higher probability that life will go our way, but has anyone been able assure that life WILL go the way they want all of the time? Jesus was nailed to a cross. Do you think that was on his personal agenda? The point I am making is that we are here to act, to surrender, to let the divine work through us. We are here to do our best and give up the fruits of our actions to the divine, and then let the cards fall where they may.

Many people mistake this idea of renouncing our actions to mean that they should not do anything. If nothing happens, then that is God's will. There is the thought they should renounce their work, family, obligations etc, to know God. In our current age, that is not a useful thought. If work is troubling, if family gets in the way of your decisions, or your obligations waste your time and your resources, then yes, cut them loose. Otherwise, this is a projection of your own inability to accept the moment, and to blame it on an external situation.

Real renunciation is being appropriate to the moment while letting go of attachment to the action. If your kid needs a new pair of shoes, it's appropriate to get him a pair. No need to think about it. That is what needs to occur. If your coworker is going out to lunch, and you realize you are hungry, but you didn't bring food to work, and she asks you to tag along, that is appropriate. Who needs to think about it? If you have a terrible disease and need treatment, do some research, find out what would help out, and if you want to live, take action. If you don't like your spouse anymore and you don't have much in common or are not supportive of each other's lifestyle, it may be time for counseling or moving on. Make a decision and let it go. You can never look back and say, "Well, if I had only done that..."

Even if you had only done 'that', no one can say what the outcome would've been.

To avoid useless thinking and endless worrying and begin more fully moving into a state of tranquility, follow these steps:

1) Look at the situation you are in.

2) Ask, "what is appropriate for me to do here?"

3) Based on the information you have, and the inner guidance that is available to you, make a decision.

4) Act on the decision.

5) Let the result be what it is. You can't control that. That's the way it is, so make some peace with it.

6) Move on to the next moment.

7) Repeat.

Now, you might be focused on step #3, specifically the part that talks about accessing your inner guidance. This is a very important part of the whole process, and here are some good points to remember about how this works:

- The same intelligence that organizes the trillions of cells in your body, and the spinning and whirling of the countless galaxies guides your actions.

- Inspiration and inner guidance is nothing special, mystical or flashy. There are no bells and whistles. If you think there are, that is the mind needing something interesting to pay attention to.

- The more you pay attention to your inner guidance, the more active it becomes.

- The less you pay attention to inner guidance and the more willful you are about needing to think things through, the less active is the inner guidance.

Learning to Access Your Inner Guidance

First, you can meditate every day. That will allow you to detach from your mind and your thinking process so you can become aware of the vast stillness from which the inner guidance comes. Then as you go about your day, if you need to make a decision, you can remember what it was like to be in the silence, and then ask, "What is appropriate here?"

Now, the response will not be a thought. If you ask the question, and you are greeted with a flurry of thoughts resembling a list of multiple choice answers, ignore them. Remember the silence, and ask again. Then wait. You will find that the inner guidance comes out of nowhere. It does not come in the form of a thought. It comes as an impulse. The impulse feels natural. When someone calls your phone you don't think about it, you just immediately decide to ignore it or answer it. When someone asks what your name is, again you don't think about it, you just decide to say your name. That's the kind of feeling that the inner guidance resembles. It is immediate and natural.

The more you trust yourself to live in this way, the better decisions you will be making. You will not be relying on the limited information in your mind to make decisions, you will be merged with your infinite nature and allowing the natural expression of that nature to come through. Note, I did not say that everything will work out exactly as you expect it to. To think that is a waste of time and a way of maintaining unreasonable expectations. A well informed man once said, "Not even the very wise can see all ends." And he said it for a reason!

Your Purpose Is Found in Your Vision

We have a vision of life. Each of us has ideas about how life works, why people are the way they are, what an ideal life looks like. In our consciousness we have moods, and thoughts and memories we constantly entertain. These are the threads of the fabric of our vision.

Do you want to know what your vision of life is?

Look at the people around you.

Look at the moods and feelings you habitually have.

Look at what you do with your time.

Look at the thoughts you allow yourself to think.

This is your vision. You see it outside, but you only see it there, because that is the way you believe life is, that is your internal faith in the world. This is usually the hardest thing to swallow, because it can be EXTREMELY hard to change. This depends on how invested we are in this vision. Again, meditation is so important, because over time, if we do it right, we eventually get to see that we are NOT our thoughts, moods, actions, friends, etc. If we are not these things, it is easier to change them, because they do not define us. If you want to know your purpose, it is sustaining your vision.

Remember, we are infinite. The real us is not bound by time, or space, or circumstance.

We have free will. To think that there is a divine being in the sky proclaiming that "such and such" should happen, is another way of skirting our responsibility and once more projecting the source of our experiences somewhere outside of us. Our fate, our purpose, is just the accumulation of our past thoughts, actions, and states of consciousness. God is infinite. That means there are infinite possibilities. ANYTHING CAN HAPPEN. While embodied, we have a choice in regards to what part of our infinity we want to experience.

We've talked about giving up the fruits of our actions and letting results be what they may. Yet I also encourage you to live a dynamic life, making choices and moving in the direction you want to go. This can create a bit of dissonance. It can inspire someone to ask, "Well, if I can't control the results, why should I try to do anything at all?"

As my spiritual teacher once said to me over lunch, "You will always be somewhere in Infinity." So let your purpose be to build your ideal vision. As you persist, and give your vision attention and are skillful and mindful as you go, your vision will become a reality. Worrying about your mistakes, and thinking about the results doesn't help you get there. It is your intention, fortified by your actions, thoughts, feelings and faith, that creates it.

Yogananda once said, that within failure is the best time to sow the seeds of success. This is because if you fail at an endeavor, you have just burnt off some of the force of your past actions that were supportive of failure. When you fail, and you get up and keep moving toward your goal, you are taking actions and setting intentions for success. To continue in this way, eventually, the power of your actions dedicated to being successful in an endeavor will become stronger than your past actions towards failure. Then success in a given endeavor becomes the norm. It's all about the interplay between your past and present actions.

Fate is the accumulation of your past actions and modes of being. You create your future fate by the persistence of your present actions and modes of being.

Creating Your Vision and Purpose

Now that you have had a chance to do some reflecting on your mental concepts of purpose and life, let's get right down determining your role in life and how that role is determined.

Step 1 – Make peace with the role you have been playing up until now. This may take some reflection, some therapy, or just a moment's notice. What ever you need to do, do it.

Step 2 – Acknowledge that your head might be filled with thoughts, ideas, intentions, successes and failures of others you have encountered. Decide if you want to keep listening to the stuff in your head. Remember, the people that you have allowed to influence your sense of self are just like you. So there is nothing special about their input that you need to pay attention to unless you want to. Even if they are extremely persuasive people, that doesn't make their insights more pertinent, it just means they are better at making an impression and being persuasive.

Step 3 – Begin to use your imagination. Brainstorm. Get out a sheet of paper and write at the top MY VISION OF LIFE. Then make a list of 100 specific things you would be doing, ways you would be feeling, the types of people you would be interacting with if you were living your vision in this moment. Do not stop until you reach 100.

Step 4 – Face your fears. Look at your vision of life. Take another sheet of paper. Look at each of the 100 items individually. Write down what would need to change in your life to make this so. Then write down why this scares you.

Step 5 – Looking at your fears, take another sheet of paper. Now beside each fear, list what the pros and cons are of remaining immobilized by this fear.

Step 6 – Decide if your vision is worth it to you. If it is, proceed to step 7. If it's not, start over or revise your vision. But remember, you will get exactly what you settle for.

Step 7 – Look at the list of actions you need to take to experience your vision. Make a discipline of doing at least one thing every day, that will make your vision a reality. Find pictures of people who have accomplished the same thing. Keep those pictures somewhere you can see them often. Read biographies of people who have accomplished this similar vision. In this way, you will be attuning to their state of consciousness and accessing the support of that state. Avoid people who are unsupportive in their thoughts and actions. Don't talk about your vision to anyone, unless you have a mentor that can guide you. Keep your energy for actually doing what it takes to birth your vision.

Step 8 – Let go of the results of your actions, and persist until your vision is as natural as the current vision of your life is. Let your purpose be manifesting this vision.

CHAPTER 5

GRACE AND SPIRITUAL PRACTICE

First meditate and feel the divine Presence; then do your work saturated with the consciousness of God. If you do this you will never become tired. If you work for your Divine Beloved, your life will be filled with love and strength. -Paramahansa Yogananda

Your body and your life are filled with grace. I would even go so far as to say they are pure grace. Many people are not aware of this truth. They struggle and search and pray and beg to feel and to know grace. All the while, the same grace they are searching for is the very thing that holds their form together and is the very essence of their being.

We meditate to become more fully aware of this presence of grace within our lives. It is always there, but we have forgotten how to feel and experience it. We listen to our minds and the thoughts of others, and we become enamored with the chase and pursuit of happiness, then we miss what is primary. We forget that we are just playing a game of cat and mouse with happiness, and that when we don't feel like playing the game anymore we can stop chasing it, and just accept it.

Through meditation we are learning to restrain our restless striving for something better. We are training our attention to stay still. For we can only experience that which we are. Once we have learned to be still, then we know stillness. Once we can learn to be an instrument of grace in the world, then we learn to experience grace directly. Grace is always active, and in stillness can we perceive it, for it is subtle, and the noise of the world can easily drown out the sensation of its presence.

One very powerful way to experience the divine presence and grace in your life is to quit thinking of yourself and give your full attention to serving others without thought of reward. Now, some of you may say that you have done this and that it has worn you down and made you bitter because you were not appreciated for your efforts. The problem is that you were hoping for appreciation. This is not how the divine works. It gives love unconditionally to the sinner, the saint, the beggar, the rich person, the clerk, the president, the drug addict, the murderer, the meditator, or the pencil maker. They are all the same.

To know grace, which is to know the divine, requires that we completely forget our selves. This self of which I am referring is the little you that has its story, its likes and dislikes, its preferences, etc. That self is fiction anyway. When we give our attention to the fiction, we experience limitation. If we can learn to turn our attention to the unlimited divine, then that is what we experience. Working as the divine, we can never know bitterness or resentment or tiredness, because we have all the energy we need, **because we are all the energy we need.**

We are not here to save up all our love and grace for a rainy day, but to learn to spend it freely, and give it away. Then we realize we are the very river of grace that we have always been, and grace no longer becomes a question, it becomes its own reality. In this way, we learn to exist as a transcendent being. We can be in the world when we choose, playing our role, whatever that may entail. We can also pull back from our personality and function as our immortal spiritual nature, free of limitation, clouded judgments, or lack of resources.

Exercise #1

Give Up The Fruits of Your Actions

Over the next several days, make a commitment every night before you go to bed and every morning when you wake up, that no matter what activity you have to perform throughout the day, you are doing it as an offering to your concept of the Divine. You are not doing it for money, or for thanks, or for appreciation. You are creating a gift for the Divine by means of your actions.

Accept that you are truly creating something, a gift, for the Divine Presence. I know if I were preparing a gift for God, I would give it my fullest attention. I would imbue it with love, I would smile as I worked, because God can feel the intentions sent into any object by way of our thinking. So no matter what you are doing, give it your fullest attention and do your best to imbue it with presence, love, care, and peace. Even if you can only do that poorly at first, in this regard, it truly is the thought that counts.

If you have to perform an activity for a coworker, spouse, child, friend, mother-in-law, keep the thought in the back of your mind, that the divine is animator of the personality of this person. Do not perform the actions for the personality, do it for the divine presence behind the personality. See only the divine in everyone you work for. No discrimination is allowed. Their actions, whether you judge them to be excellent, poor, good or bad, is just the role God is playing through them. Ignore that. See only the light behind their eyes, even if you have to try exceptionally hard to imagine that.

Step 1 – Every night before you go to sleep, have a talk with yourself. Talk about all the ways you will work to serve the divine tomorrow, by writing that report, meeting with that patient, paying that bill, scrubbing that floor, etc. If you have to work with unpleasant people, give your self a pep talk about how you are going to change your perceptions, and no matter how hard it might be, you are going to see the light of God behind the personality and work only for that, not for the personality.

Step 2 – When you wake up in the morning, before you even get out of bed, reaffirm your commitment to this process. If you have to, tell your self that you are not a child, and that you know this is good for you (at least if you want to experience tranquility and grace in your life), and that "you are going to do it and you are going to like it!"

Step 3 – Get out of bed, and keep your attention, as best you can, on every action. Begin your work creating Gifts for the Divine as often as you can. As you shower, you are bathing the body of the divine. As you eat, you are recharging the body to do the work ahead. As you drive, you are driving through the divine presence.

Remember, we become what we think about. If we turn every thought of every action to the Divine, what will we become? Let me know when you find out.

I know it would be great if all of this was easy, and maybe it is for you, but I'll admit it wasn't for me, and it's not for a lot of people. Why? Because unless you are born with an unyielding sense of optimism and joy, it can be hard to maintain these kinds of exercises. So it takes work. But you see, when we have recreated our 'incarnated' self to experience this kind of living, then we have the power to continue creating in this way, and we have the power to remain in Grace, because it was by our own efforts that we turned towards grace. We were not wantonly blown into an experience of the divine by fate, we built up our divine muscles and said, "I'm going to climb that mountain!" And now you know how to climb it, so if you ever fall off, or go down to the village for a while, you still know how to climb it!

Going to Heaven, Hell or Beyond?
You Decide.

Many yogic spiritual texts affirm the assertion that heaven and hell is not a permanent state we go to for our failures or successes. They say that heaven is just the accumulation of our past intentions to experience a heaven-like state, and hell is an accumulation of our misdeeds that will allow us, at some point, to experience that state. After the energy behind our intentions to experience heaven and hell loses momentum, we come back to where we started! This is why, yogic texts express the release of cravings and hopes and fears, so that we may no longer give attention to the temptations of heaven, and the sufferings of hell. We go beyond them. Neither do we yearn for what we consider fantastic, nor do we run away from that which bothers us. We do what is appropriate in the moment, and then we are free to act consciously, in Divine Grace, to do what needs to be done.

Here are a few formulas you may find useful in this regard:

- If you want to go to heaven after death or have a heaven-like experience on earth, be happy right now. Work unflinchingly for the benefit of others. Do not think about yourself beyond providing for your basic and moderate needs. Live every day for God.

- If you want to experience (or continue experiencing) hell after death or on earth, remain in an attitude of resentment towards your past. Nurture the past wrongs and hurts you have endured and inflicted on others. Steal. Hurt people. Think only of what you can get out of every experience.

- If you want to go beyond heaven and hell and know your true unconditioned eternal nature, and the need to maintain a certain state to experience peace and tranquility, give up your fears and desires. Let go of the concepts of heaven and hell. Practice a spiritual technique that quiets your being. Learn to exist in that stillness in meditation and as you go about your duties in the world. Learn to do what is appropriate in the moment, beyond your judgment of good and bad. In this way your karma will exhaust itself, and no matter where you find your self in eternity, you can smile, free of the fears of losing your reason to smile, and you can smile, free of the attachment to smiling!

Now, in most cases, you would first focus on experiencing the heaven-like state as mentioned above and let go of the hell-like state and the actions that take you there. Then once you are stable in that state of consciousness, you move beyond it to transcending attachments to both heaven and hell.

However, as mentioned before, I don't like to waste time, and this isn't a course on getting into heaven, and I'd like to advise pursuing the last bullet point above. Why? Because once you are in a state of grace, it doesn't matter what happens on the "outside." You know you are just playing your role in the divine drama. Established in that grace beyond fear and desire, you can take off and put on the mask of your personality as often as you like. You are then free. You are free, you can relax and be tranquil, because you know what you are beyond all conditioning. You are then a transcendent being!

Transcendence in Your Daily Life

People who report having transcendent experiences almost always affirm having a sense of peace and familiarity about the episode. The deep stillness they sense is described as being something they have known all along, not as something new or strange or foreign. It feels like coming home.

At first, on the spiritual path, we may be enamored with strange perceptions during meditation, such as radiant lights or perceptions of astral landscapes, or feelings of bliss and ecstasy. We may long for visions of Gods, Goddesses, Angels, or Ascended masters. Our imagination will provide them of course, but in reality, this is entertainment no different than what you get at the movies or on your computer. Anything that you can perceive is "out there", and we want you to be "in here" existing freely as your Self. We want you to know what you are, rather than searching for interesting phenomena.

As a person goes through the stages of spiritual awakening, it becomes more and more ordinary. Gone are the desires to seek a sense of completion or fulfillment through something external. If it is appropriate, a tranquil spiritually aware person can sit for long periods of time, simply being. To someone hypnotized by the mind and addicted to sense stimulation, this seems outrageously ludicrous. Isn't the act of spiritual awakening meant to lift you out of the human condition and into a divine condition? Yes it is, but the divine condition is not a glorified human condition, as our minds would like to believe.

Spend some time in nature. Watch the wind blowing through the trees as they sway back and forth, or observe the wind rolling over the long grass of late summer. See how the sun and moon cross the sky, and the stars shine as if eternally fixated in the heavens. Nature can show the consistent tranquility of simply being.

See how there is no clinging to the past or expectation of the future in nature. When the rose blooms, it is beautiful. Its scent fills the air. As the season passes, it fades, and dies. There is no argument. The Spring will come again. Even if it doesn't for this particular rose bush, it will for some other plant. There is no need to worry about which plant. It does not matter what names or forms are given to the rising and falling waves on the ocean of consciousness, because it is all the same ocean.

The clearer we realize what reality is, the less words we need to direct us there. The sage Vasistha said that "words are only used to instruct the ignorant [the one who is spiritually asleep]. Once there is knowledge, words are no longer needed." This is why we begin on our spiritual path embracing a specific teaching, teacher or tradition. We start with a concept of what it is supposed to be like, and then we practice what we are taught. As we grow, our concepts change, until eventually we outgrow all concepts. Once we are beyond concepts we are 'in reality'. The specific practices we adopt are like the crucible that is used to forge steel. Once the blade is made, then it has only to do its job.

I'd like to share a few experiences of how obsession with spiritual practice can negate the very thing we are trying to accomplish, and block transcendence.

A few years into my studies as a Kriya Yogi, I had maintained my zeal for meditating at least one hour every morning and when possible another hour later in the day. One

Saturday, we were hosting a party on our 13 acre farm. The plan was to have lots of homemade food, and a large bonfire. I loved to cook and to build big fires. The party was a good excuse.

That morning I rose and meditated and did a short hatha yoga routine. I then decided to go out into the cool morning and begin gathering firewood and kindling for the night's fire. As I tromped through the tall grass, and scoured the forest, I began thinking, "If I hurry, I can go back inside and meditate for another hour, because that would do me good." This thought began to grow, and I became more anxious to go back inside and meditate.

After I had gathered most of the wood we needed, I stopped breaking the twigs off of the piece of wood I was working on, and looked up. A cool breeze came across my face. I saw the sun creating rainbows in the radiant dew drops on the grass. I could smell the sweet earth. A peace descended on me and I realized that the entire time I had been worrying about going back in to meditate longer, I could've been 'being' completely present in the Divine grace that was all around me. For the rest of the day I remained in that state, tranquil, internally still, while actively preparing for the night's festivities.

On another occasion, I had been going about my day doing normal self-employed business office duties. With each action, whether I was writing an email, driving to the post office, researching a chart, I noticed that I was always waiting and hoping for something. For what!?! I was waiting for the action I was doing to be over, because I could be better using my time reading spiritual literature or meditating. I was hoping I could get everything done so I'd have more time to reflect on life and my relationship to God. So I could spend more time in the peace of nature. Ridiculous!

What was the result of this waiting and hoping? I was not aware that in every step, in every breath, in every moment I was experiencing life, I was experiencing Divine Grace. I was labeling certain actions as spiritual and certain actions as mundane, and thereby creating a separation in my Self. I had to strive to make more time to do those spiritual things, while enduring all the useless mundane things I needed to accomplish to provide for my self. I was creating a strain that didn't need to be there, and wasting my energy in useless judgmental thought patterns about what the present "should" be like!

From that point forward I committed myself to allowing each moment to be as it is, no matter the quality. I would no longer allow myself to waste the precious experiences of this life wishing them away because they didn't fit my expectations exactly as I had planned. I would, of course, keep my intention set on living the life that was ideal for me. If I found myself in an unpleasant situation, I would remove myself from it. If action needed to be taken to change an outcome, I would do it. But when things didn't work out, no matter the efforts I made, I would relax, pay attention, and let it pass, as all things will. It was in this way, that grace became apparent behind all experiences.

The two experiences mentioned above had the effect of changing my life. I learned to notice when I was waiting for 'this moment', the one I judged as unspiritual to be over, that I was really wasting my life. I learned that no matter what I was doing, it didn't really matter how I felt about it, it still had to be done. Labeling it as a waste of time, was just labeling life itself as a waste of time. To think

I should be meditating, when really I should be working or interacting with the world of form, was affirming that I clearly did not accept the truth that "God is all things, manifest and unmanifest". I wanted God, but only in a certain way, and so the grace I experienced in life was just as limited.

I learned that we make up stories in our heads about what life should be like, and then when life doesn't live up to those expectations we are disappointed. I learned to stop telling myself stories, at least 90 percent of the time, about what I was experiencing, and to just experience it.

When this happened, life blossomed. Gone were the crushing thoughts of expectations, false ideas of how things should be. What was left, was every moment, new. What had the chance to come forth in my awareness was that we live in an eternity and it doesn't matter so much if the waves of eternity are constantly perfect. What matters is that we know how to ride those waves, that we know how to really jump into the amazing waves, and that we know when and how to lay back and let the so-so ones pass.

Mahavatar Babaji said, "Few know that the kingdom of heaven extends fully to this physical world." Yogananda said, "Banish the idea that spiritual and material realities are separate." I would like to encourage you to do the same. When it is time to meditate, pray, be with your spiritual teacher, or read inspirational literature do so. When it is time to work in the world, meet people, wash your car, tell someone to get out of your way, or buy someone pizza, do so. Know that no matter what you are doing, you are in your right place in the divine drama, and don't be too attached to the outcome. Hold your vision and your intention and move forward, then let the seeds of grace sprout and grow on their own time.

CHAPTER 6

ABSOLVING YOUR PAST

Forget the past. The vanished lives of all men are dark with many shames. Human conduct is ever unreliable until anchored in the Divine. Everything in future will improve if you are making a spiritual effort now. -Sri Yukteswar

The universe is vast, both in time and in space. We cannot know with one hundred percent certainty whether the judgments we pronounce on our own and other's actions are correct, because we cannot see all the results of an action as it stretches through time. You may have noticed that sometimes, terrible events turn out to lead to a very positive result, while sometimes events that we deem as good and wholesome lead to ruin. Our ideal is to live the best we can in the present, and let the infinite divine consciousness take care of the rest.

There is an intelligence that permeates all, that is beyond the mind, that is beyond our imagined (although useful) moral codes. We cannot know it with the mind. We can only experience it directly. Tuned into and responsive to this intelligence, there is no need for thought. We function at a level of subtler development. In this way, there are no mistakes, only the working of the divine consciousness. Releasing attachment to the past clears the mental radio, so we can more easily tune our dial to the divine consciousness.

When we are identified with a human point of view, we experience limitation. That is the nature of human consciousness, to work from a limited viewpoint, through a finite personality. Anyone caught in the trap of intellectualism or philosophy will have great difficulty processing the concept that there is a power and intelligence beyond the mind.

The solution is not to throw out philosophy or intellectualism or reason or the ability to use common sense. All of these have their place just as a fork is used to eat salad and a spoon for eating soup. The main solution is to accept the usefulness and limitations of our minds and then learn to step out of the mind. Done properly, this brings us into direct experience of the creative intelligence that successfully animates all life while simultaneously spinning the cosmos, all at once. (Which, you know, is quite a feat if you've ever tried it!) We are then free of our history and free to live spontaneously in the divine consciousness.

Our past experiences and our history are very useful when properly digested. Having memories of the past enables us to function in this time-space continuum as an individual. It allows us to play a role, and to accomplish our purposes. We remember where we have been, what we have done, who we have met. From this we are able to learn what promotes or hinders our worthwhile purposes. We can then choose the proper path in life, knowing what to avoid and what to seek out.

If our mental digestion is off, then we become confused. Memories of past actions, thoughts, and feelings become a jumble. We then feel we have to keep thinking about these confusing bits of information until we can make sense of them. All the while, we are still moving through time and space and accumulating even more thoughts, memories, feelings, etc. The mental indigestion just keeps getting worse, because we never stop the incoming flow of impressions!

This is a difficult state of affairs, because everything we experience is based on how the divine light of consciousness projects through the film reel of the mind. The more chaotic, bloated, and uncomfortable the mind becomes, so too does our life experience. When the mind can no longer manage, it breaks down. Mental distress becomes pronounced, and more difficulties arise in the life situation.

There are a number of ways to remedy this. One is daily internalized meditation. By giving attention to the breath or a mantra for 20 minutes a day, while ignoring all else, the mind has a chance to digest and clear out old data. The second most helpful way of dealing with mental indigestion is to have an intentional conscious review of your most immediate past once a day, or at least two-three times a week. The third technique, which can be done at all times, is being fully in the present without judgment.

Meditation Clears Up Mental Indigestion

You may have noticed by now that when you sit to meditate, often you do not instantly enter into a quiet space. You may find that the song you heard two hours ago, or the email your mother sent last night, or the big project you have at work, or the current credit card balance are all on your mind. You may even find that you are still having flashes of incidents that occurred twenty years ago, or are still thinking the same repetitious negative self-talk you had going through your head since you were ten years old.

What you are experiencing is the vast reservoir of the past that you have been storing in your attic all this time. When you sit to meditate, essentially, you are pulling down the steps that lead up the attic and are becoming aware of just how much junk you've been stowing away. As you meditate, you remove bits and pieces of this junk, one day at a time.

Some people store more than others, and so it takes different amounts of time for everyone to clean out their inner space. The thing you need to know, is that it's never going to get cleaned up until you start taking the time to do it. Your time is 20 minutes a day of meditation, and if you can sit comfortably for longer, sit for longer.

As they say in the Yoga Sutras, "Spiritual progress is in accord with one's level of intensity, and this can be mild, medium, or very intensive." By intensity I am not encouraging you to be a fanatic, and thinking you have to meditate all the time. I am encouraging you to practice all three of the techniques listed in this lesson regularly, so you can move from cleaning up your mess, to being a clear vessel for the divine consciousness to flow through you.

Once you can leave your past behind, you can focus on what you can do in the present. This is what it means to be anchored in the divine. The divine is not in the past, it is only now.

Intentional Conscious Thought Review

When we try to meditate or even when we are going to bed at night, the flurry of thoughts can be very annoying and persistent. The thoughts can prevent you from getting a good night's sleep. They can prevent you from having a deep and powerful meditation.

This occurs because there is a part of you that thinks these thoughts are very important, and that you really should be thinking about them rather than wasting your time sleeping or trying to experience the divine presence within through meditation. If you have this problem, the best thing you can do is take some time to intentionally think about everything that's on your mind, rather than letting the thoughts think you!

What does this look like? When you are going to bed, and you notice the flurry of thoughts, acknowledge that they are there. Then lay in bed and stare at the ceiling or close your eyes, and rather than letting the thoughts run wild, use your will power to actively think about what you've got running through your mind.

Here is an example to help show what I mean:

Chuck is lying in bed trying to sleep. Here are the thoughts that are running wild through his head...

"I hope Audrey doesn't find that credit card bill...When was the last time I changed the oil in the car...I can't believe Sally got fired...Maybe we can have crab legs

tomorrow...I have to remember to cut the grass...That investment is doing really well...What's that noise...We can go camping this weekend...That chicken didn't sit well with me...It's been five years, and I still haven't heard from my uncle Bill...When I get back to the office I'm not going to take insults from anyone anymore..."

This is an example of passive thinking. In this situation, the thoughts are thinking Chuck, and so Chuck suffers at their hands.

An alternative situation would be if, while lying in bed, Chuck became aware of all of this mental indigestion, and then decided he wanted to get a really good night's sleep. He would then do the following...

"OK. Enough of all this useless chatter. Let's think about this stuff and then let it go. All this stuff is going through my head, so a part of me thinks I need to think about it. So I'm going to think about it with intention.

"I will pay off the credit card and shred the bill first thing tomorrow morning."

"Next."

"Let's see, there are 46,000 miles on the car. I got the oil changed at 45,000. So I've got 2,000 more miles to go."

"Next thought."

"Sally got fired. So what. She was lazy anyway."

"Next."

"No more fried chicken before bed. Crab legs will be good for dinner tomorrow."

"Next."

"Uncle Bill was crazy. Who cares that I haven't seen him in five years."

"Ok mind, what else do you want to think about?"

--No thoughts arise--

"Are you sure? It's only been 45 seconds, and I'm not tired yet."

"Did you order flowers for your anniversary?" Thinks the mind."

"Oh no...oops...I mean, tomorrow at lunch I will order flowers for Audrey."

--No thoughts arise--

"Ok. Now we've thought about everything you thought was important, I'm going to sleep."

(Chuck then falls quickly to sleep.)

This activity moves one from the endless stream of consciousness thoughts, to actively, thought by thought, thinking about what is on one's mind. Then all thoughts have been reviewed, the mind can relax and sleep can happen without all of that mental clutter. If you are going to be thinking, do it actively. The more actively you think, the less unconscious baggage you will create. The mind will become sharper and a better tool for you. Rather than running like an old clunker that hardly ever gets any attention, and makes all kinds of noise, it will run like a fancy sports car that is well-cared for.

The same applies to meditation. If you find you have a stream of thoughts that never quit, pay attention to what you are thinking about. Then say to your self, "Ok. I'm going to actively think about this stuff right now, so I don't have to think about it during meditation." Once you have, then move on to meditation practice.

A final point that might be helpful for you, is to have a note book beside your meditation spot, or beside your bed. I've often found that when I start to meditate, the thoughts that get in my way, are all the things I have to accomplish through out the day. Or sometimes I get lots of ideas about new projects in meditation. I then continue thinking about these things, as though I'm going to forget. So by having a notebook beside me, I can immediately write down what's on my mind, and I know it's there for when I'm done meditating or to review tomorrow morning. This way I don't have to keep thinking about it. I can then meditate freely.

Life Review

Beyond the level of repetitious simple thoughts, one thing that can really hinder our movement into a state of tranquility is obsession with the past. This can come in the form of longing for the good times that have faded away, to still harboring confusion about something terrible that was done to you or that you did to someone else.

We have to remember that we cannot do anything at all about the past. We cannot change what occurred. We cannot bring back what has been lost. No matter how hard we try, even if we could align the external environment to mimic something we remembered long ago, our internal states are different and so we would still lack fulfillment. Terrible deeds cannot be altered, nor can we change a person's behavior toward us because it was unjust.

We can, however, make peace with reality. To think that something shouldn't have happened, or to wish it hadn't happened, does not change the fact that it did. Thinking things should've been different and wishing for a different past is one of the biggest wastes of time any of us can engage. We do this, because on some level, we have a fantasy in our head that says, "Life should have happened this way, because that's how all the fairy tales go..." What is missing in this process, is the acknowledgment that we don't live in a fairy tale.

You made a mistake and hurt someone. You were young and stupid. That's not an excuse, but it is a reality. If you regret it, and do it again, then you are still stupid. That's a reality. If you reflect on the situation, realize you were young and stupid, admit that you learned from your mistake and that you know better now, then all you can do is live with that wisdom. Living from this wisdom, your future is much better than the past. Besides, we are not walking into the past, we are walking into the future. So if you are going to focus on something, making a better future, is the way to go, and this is based on your present choices, not your past.

If someone has been terrible to us, we can forgive them, and then decide that we will not subject ourselves to that kind of treatment anymore. Most of the excessive thoughts that come from being mistreated may stem from a fear that it will happen again. If we have been mistreated, the best way to not waste any more of your thought force is to decide with finality: "Yes, that was a bad situation. And I'm not going to repeat it. If someone starts to do that to me again, I will either stop them, or leave." Now that you've made a decision, you don't have to think about it any more. Once again, your future is better because of the action you are taking in the present, that was based on a learning experience from the past.

Since we are focusing on being realistic, we do have to remember that certain thoughts or activities have been entertained for so long, that sometimes there is a delay between when we decide to start thinking and living differently in the present and the results of our new, useful, choices. If you have been eating a bag of chips every night and drinking four cans of soda a day for forty years, chances are that deciding to drink water and eat celery instead is going to take a little while to show its results. Similarly, if you have been thinking thoughts of poverty or dwelling on traumas for decades, you can decide to stop immediately, but it may take some time for your life to adjust to the new input of feeling "provided for" and that relationships can be fun and joyful. However, the other option is to continue doing what you've been doing and thereby prolonging the problems you may have.

You can use the following technique to help digest your past history. It can be used before a meditation session, or even two to three times a week before you go to sleep.

Step 1 – Bring your attention to your third eye center, the space between your eyebrows. With your eyes closed, slightly look up into your skull, as though you are looking into your mind.

Step 2 – Begin breathing steadily. Your breath can be a little deeper than usual, but you want to be breathing comfortably. Consistency and steadiness is the key.

Step 3 – You are now going to review your past 24-48 hours. Start with where you are right now. Right now you are sitting in your chair getting ready to meditate.

Step 4 – Actively think about the last thing you did. If it was brushing your teeth. Remember brushing your teeth, and mentally say, "I brushed my teeth".

Step 5 – Rewind again, thinking about what you did before brushing your teeth. "I watched the news." Now remember the images that stuck out in your brain from the news program. Just acknowledge them and then keep going.

Step 6 – Rewind again. What did you do before that? State what you did, mentally. Then review the memories that come up for you around that activity.

Step 7 – Continue this process until you have thought about everything you experienced that you can remember over the last 24-48 hours. Then proceed with your meditation practice.

Every now and again, you may need to take some time to sit for even longer and then review your entire life, as much as you can remember. Start with where you are in this very moment, and begin rewinding the picture show of your day, reviewing each incident, until you lose the ability to remember little details, then start moving back in bigger chunks. Review weeks that stick out in your mind, certain days and experiences, etc, until you can't remember anything else. Just do your best to move backwards in chronological order. Then let it go, and continue with your meditation.

The more often you do this, while objectively observing the process, admitting all the good and bad stuff that happened in your life, the wiser you will become. Your mental baggage will become lighter and lighter. Your meditations will become deeper. Your sleep will become easier. Your interactions with the world will become more pleasant, because on each review of your life, you will see what went well and what went wrong, and you will avoid the problematic components more readily.

Our history only defines us so much as we identify with it. Whatever we identify with, that is what we will become. If we identify with the past, we will repeat it, and we will become a relic. If we have a vision of how we'd like to be, and we identify with that in the present, our past can only hold us back so long, until the force of our present actions overcomes the force of choices we have left behind.

Being Present Without Judgment

One of the hardest things for people to do, is to exist in a situation while remaining internally quiet. Even if we are only going for a walk down the hill and back, we can't help but to keep up the mental chatter. "Oh look, that's a blue bird. How wonderful that flower smells. Who forgot to scoop their dog's poop? I bet it was Jim from down the street. Isn't the sun hot!" And so it goes. Put us in a situation that runs counter to our beliefs and just watch the mind jump into action! "Can you believe that person cut me off like that? It's just not right that Paul makes more money than me even though we do the same amount of work! That mugger didn't have to hit me in the face. I bet Michelle wears that perfume just to irritate me!" Here we are labeling everything.

The real beauty of the divine in every moment comes forth more readily when we are quiet and watching. Then we see the life that animates the blue bird. We feel the essence of the flower. We watch the human drama unfold in its ever changing array of activities, some pleasant, some not.

This is hard to do, because everything that happens, happens to us. If we stop labeling and judging everything, then there is nothing happening to us. We start to lose identification with our personality. This can be very scary, and hence why so few people try to be in the present moment. The wonderful thing is that when you can be fully present, witnessing what happens around you, acting appropriately without attachment to the results of your actions, then you experience wholeness and the fullness of life. Gone is the feeling that you are a little insignificant person in an endless universe, and what washes over you is the feeling that you are completely attuned to the perfection of the divine drama.

Here is how you practice being present:

Step 1 – Choose a time period for your practice. It can be 15 minutes or an hour. Pick a time when you are interacting with the world in your usual ways. So don't pick 6 AM in the morning when no one is awake. You want to make sure you are fully in the activity of the day.

Step 2 – Once your allotted time begins, become acutely aware of your environment and the thoughts your environment promotes.

Example 1: You are walking to the water cooler to get a drink. A coworker steps in front of you and fills her cup up first. In this situation you are aware of what is happening, and then you become aware of your assessment of this situation. "How rude. She saw me walking towards the cooler first." Acknowledge your judgment. Then drop your judgment. Be aware of only what is really happening.

You walked to the water cooler.

Someone stepped out in front of you.

You get your drink after they did.

That's it. Your judgment is useless, so don't waste your time.

Example 2: You are walking down the street. You see a beautiful flower in a streak of sunlight, shining through the space between two buildings. Just see the colors and the light. Don't say, "Oh my, isn't that iris lovely!" If you can just see what is there, you will see more deeply into the experience and begin to realize just how alive the present really is with divine consciousness!

Step 3 – Always acknowledge and then drop the judgment. Assess whether your judgment adds anything to the situation. I bet it doesn't. Then decide to stop wasting your energy on judgment.

Step 4 – Decide if it is appropriate to do anything about the situation. If action is appropriate, take it. If not, move on with your day. Decide at that moment if action is important, and don't keep judging if you made the right decision. Your decision is in the past. See what happens. If your decision caused a problem, decide to make a different choice next time. Then move on.

Continue this practice for your allotted time. The purpose of this exercise isn't to "stop your thoughts", although that will occur. It is to point out the uselessness of these thoughts. Once you experience that your judgments don't really change anything, it will be easier for you to let go of them. Try this at least once a day for the next two weeks.

CHAPTER 7

REALITY VS. YOUR STORY

As stated in the book *Vasistha's Yoga* there are countless universes or realities floating on a sunbeam, or in a rock, or in a speck of dust on the air. The sage Vasistha also said that our life span is only the blink of an eye to other beings of whom we are not aware. According to physics, there is the potential that existing simultaneously in our very body are untold worlds, but in a different dimension or plane of existence. Knowing this, we see that what we consider to be reality is really only a point of view we adopt to relate to the world.

Take a moment to think of the countless roles adopted around the world. You can be Hindu, Christian, Democrat, Republican, Zen, Orthodox Jewish, Yuppie, Hippie, scientist, nerd, athlete, jerk, nice person, saint, sinner, rich, poor, Southern, Northern, musician, or a combination of two or more, and the list goes on. Each person that identifies with a particular role will identify with it as though it is completely correct. Each is in their own reality and relate to the world through that lens. Think of all the arguments, wars and hurt feelings that have been caused, because people thought their point of view was the correct one.

Now obviously there has to be some kind of objective way of determining who's correct, right? No. Incorrect. Your mind wants you to think that, because the mind likes to be right and have a point to defend, so it can feel superior. The point of being tranquil and enlightened is not to defend a point. It is to "live a natural and spontaneous life contentedly." Remember that? Another quote from Vasistha. That means that rather than building up an idea in your mind of who you are and what you stand for, you decide that you will be fully present in every moment and respond appropriately to each situation as it arises, free of attachment to ideologies, roles or what you think is right.

This is not easy and it is why the world has as many religions as it does. Religion, properly understood, is good for keeping people out of trouble. It creates a set of laws and guidelines that if followed, may lead to an enlightened life, and if properly understood, will at least lead to a harmonious society that is stable and supportive. We identify with a moral code, religion or set of principles to get us moving forward on a positive path that keeps us from hurting ourselves or others. We have to remember these are very useful training wheels that must not be cast off too quickly!

Enlightened people usually live harmoniously with the world, and so killing, stealing and coveting is what they avoid naturally. They are enlightened and know what a world of hurt the retribution from those activities can cause, and so they avoid them. Enlightened people, through experience, know that spending time daily communing with the divine presence is a fount of joy and inspiration. No one has to tell them they have to do it, because they are wise enough and experienced enough to know that true joy only comes from having no investment in a transient world, but by building their joy on the immortal nature of the spirit. It's not a question of religion or law for them, it's based on experience.

The point of this discussion is to illustrate that each of us identifies with a chosen point of view. Some of those points of view are often complex and contradictory. However, it may be that at this time, in order for you to get the most out of life, you have to identify with a point of view, or a particular religion, or idea of who you are. If that is the reality of your situation, accept it and move on. If you have found that holding certain points of view only gets you in trouble or creates strife in your life and relationships, you may need to consider that it's not really worth it to identify with that idea. Some good examples include:

"My spouse should enjoy spending time with my parents."

"I should be appreciated for what I do."

"I should be able to eat a gallon of ice cream every day and not get sick."

"The house should be clean all the time."

"People should be nicer to each other."

"No one should eat meat."

"If people believed exactly as I do the world would be great."

You might like things to be a certain way, but if your reality says otherwise, remember, arguing with reality doesn't work. Reality may very well be showing you that your spouse doesn't like your parents, or that no one really cares if you are appreciated, or that the house is often messy, and some people love bacon and ribs. If so, drop these false ideas that no longer serve you and move on. Holding ideas that would be nice if they were true, but do not line up with reality is a sure way to get yourself in an unhappy space.

Remember, we are endeavoring to be tranquil and happy for no reason! Why? Because then no reason can take away our happiness.

What Does a Life in "Reality" Look Like?

When you arrive home from a hard day's work, you see the sink filled with dishes, the yard overgrown and a wreck. Immediately you think, "Dale has been home all day! Why is this place a mess?!" Then you fume and create a story of how Dale should've cleaned up the mess, which eventually leads to an argument and hurt feelings.

If you were in reality and didn't allow your mind to engage, you would've walked into this situation, seen the dishes, and realized. "The dishes needed cleaning." Then, you would've cleaned the dishes, because that was appropriate. No need for a story or ruffling of feathers. Drying the last dish, you would look out the window and see the lawn needs mowing. Walking out to the shed, you would start the lawn mower and complete the task. Then you would notice you need a bath. After taking your bath, you yawn and see your favorite spiritual book beside your bed. Taking up the book, you would read a page or two before falling to sleep happily beside your beloved Dale. The Sun rises, and you begin again, meditating, showering, eating a nice breakfast (and cleaning up the dishes) before going to work.

In this example, you see that everything you need to know, in regards to how to act and what to do is provided. No need to think about it. Just pay attention to what is before you and what is appropriate. Your stories don't help. To think that, "I am a hard worker. My family should respect me by treating me better." That is a story. You made it up. There is no reality to it. And so you see, when you are not in reality, you can invent a mess of problems.

An Experience with My Father

My parents live on a river and many of the homes on their road are summer homes. One day, a large dump truck filled with melon-sized rocks decided to turn around in the next door neighbor's drive way. It turned out that the drive way had been hollowed out underneath by an underground stream. When the truck backed into the driveway, the concrete collapsed under the extreme weight. The rocks poured out all over the drive and filled the hole. A tow truck came and removed the truck, but the gravel remained.

I was sitting on my bed listening to music and enjoying the summer breeze through my windows. My dad, as he was apt to do when I was enjoying myself, called for me to give him a hand. I thought, "Now what! I've already mowed the grass and trimmed the lawn! He's probably going to tell me what I messed up this time." As I fumed out the door, preparing for a lecture on the proper way to weed-eat, I saw him in the neighbor's driveway tossing large rocks into a wheelbarrow.

"What are you doing?" I asked, wondering why he was moving rocks out of the hole, when, in my mind, it was clearly the neighbor's responsibility, since it was their driveway.

"Take that wheelbarrow down to the river and dump it." He said.

"Why are you doing this?" I asked, making sure he understood that I thought this was a stupid idea.

"It needs done." Was all he said.

For some reason, my discontentment melted away at this. I thought to myself "he's right." There's a job that needs doing. For half a beautiful summer afternoon my father and I loaded up one wheelbarrow after another of large granite rocks and cleared out our neighbor's driveway. I could have wasted the day desiring to be back in my cool room listening to my favorite music, but I didn't. A sense of ease and purpose washed over me, and tossing granite out of a hole became a moment that was completely full, lacking in nothing.

It was that experience that showed me, that thinking someone else should be doing the work that is clearly before us is the real waste of time and energy.

Exercise #1

The day after you read this chapter, decide that you are going to do your best to be aware and alert in regards to reality. This is an extension of "Being Present Without Judgment" from the last chapter.

Step 1 – Declare to yourself once an hour, beginning as soon as you wake up. "I am going to be aware of all the 'shoulds' in my life and let them go. I am going to love Reality in whatever form it takes!"

Step 2 – As you go into your day, watch your mind.

Notice how on your drive to work, you enter a traffic jam, and you say, "Ahhh! I should be at work by 9! This traffic jam should not be happening!" Well, what's the reality? It is happening isn't it? Are you going to get to work by 9? No. Can you help it? No. So sit in traffic. What part of the stress created by arguing with reality do you enjoy? Is it really worth it?

Step 3 – As you move through your day, watch your mind.

Notice how you start to get sleepy around 2 PM. Then you say, "I got plenty of sleep last night. I shouldn't be tired." Oh no? Well what is reality telling you? Then, you start thinking of all the illnesses you might have because you are tired. All of the sudden you are creating a new reality, one with an illness in it, instead of just admitting. "Hey, I'm sleepy. I wish I wasn't, but I can't argue with reality!" Then do your best as you complete your day.

Step 4 – As you conclude your day, watch your mind.

Notice that when you come home from working hard you have a sense of entitlement about having time to yourself.

Your mind says…"Boy, I've been working hard. I can't wait to get comfy and meditate!"

Then you walk in the door and your spouse wants to know why certain bills aren't paid, or how you forgot that friends were coming for dinner, or why you aren't more affectionate, understanding and appreciative.

Your mind says…"What is going on? I shouldn't have to deal with this, doesn't he understand that I've had a busy day? I shouldn't have to deal with this!"

You don't have to deal with it. That is true. You can blow your loved one off. But that has its own consequences. Reality is in your face, in the form of your spouse, and "should" does not play a role. **You were identified with your false prediction of what the evening was going to be like, rather than waiting to see what the Reality is.** Remember, Reality always wins. Even if you try to ignore it, it still wins.

Step 5 – Repeat this exercise one day a week. As you get better, start adding a day until you are able to do it for a full seven days in a row. Then take note of how much more pleasant your life becomes.

Consequences

CONSEQUENCES! Most people don't like this word. It reminds them of being punished as a child. It makes them feel limited and bound. What they don't realize is that just as there are laws of nature, there are laws that extend throughout all of creation and through all experience.

Once you can make peace with consequences you are in a much better place in the world. Why? Because then you can make fairly sound decisions after weighing the consequences of your actions. Then you don't have to complain, either out loud or mentally, about the results of your actions. You knew the possibility of certain results occurring.

A man once said that 9 out 10 businesses fail. When another man heard this, he said to himself, "Ok, so I am committing to starting 10 businesses, knowing that at least one is probably going to work." Many of his businesses failed, but then one succeeded and now he's working well and enjoying the process.

Another man heard the remark, "9 out 10 businesses fail", and decided not to start any business, because of the potential for failure. He also went on to complain about how it was impossible to start a business.

Another man heard the same remark and tried three times, each business failing, but then gave up for fear that the fourth would as well. He decided that all the failure ruined his bank account and health.

Which one of these men stayed in Reality?

Take note of all the things you attempt in your life, well aware of the possibility of failure and success. Then be aware of how you pull your hair out and moan, when the failure possibility kicks in. You knew it was possible to fail, so why are you surprised?

Do you use light bulbs? Well, guess how many trials it took to get the first light bulb to work correctly? Estimates state that Thomas Edison went through around 10,000 trials to get the light bulb to work. Was it worth it?

This may seem harsh, but the reality is, failure is a possibility in all circumstances, as is success. Yogic teachings states that the yogi is not elated with success or failure, but sees all circumstances as an expression of the divine. When you can give yourself permission to live like that, the tranquility you so long for, when you weren't identified with a limited personality who has to win all time, that tranquility will come rushing back to you.

This is a very different way to live than what people usually teach us from birth. But as you can tell, what we are taught doesn't always work out so well when put into practice.

Very few understand this secret of complete freedom and spiritual liberation. If you are going to be free, you can't pick and choose what you are going to be free from. If you want to be free, completely and totally, you have to choose to be free of the attachment to things working out exactly as you planned, as well. This is not to say that you do not try to be successful, it only means that you are not attached to success or failure.

We need to remember that there are a number of factors that we can control in regards to experiencing success in line with Reality. We can improve our knowledge about certain topics. We can maintain a positive attitude and be receptive to bursts of intuition that will quicken our progress. We can ask other people who have been successful and learn from them. All of these methods will help us and we are not alone. Yet, we do have to be discriminative in the process.

Changing Your Interaction With Reality

Reality is like a mirror. It reflects what you put in front of it. Put thoughts or ideologies of one kind or another in front of it, and it will give you a reason to believe those thoughts and ideologies are true.

Change those thoughts and ideologies and the experience will change. Remember, reality by itself is just reality. Reality plus a certain thought or idea, becomes that thought. The equations looks like this...

> *Reality (consciousness) + nothing (no conditioning) = Reality*
>
> *Reality (or consciousness) + a certain idea*
>
> *= That idea*

From a mystical level, to truly experience reality requires a complete and total relinquishment of conceptualization. Now you might think that if you don't have concepts, you won't be able to experience anything or that nothing would exist. Well, a rock can experience its rockness, and can be broken, and made wet, and made hot, etc. But it's still just a rock. Calling it a rock, doesn't change its reality. The rock doesn't need the concept of broken, wet, or hot, to experience those things. Just like you don't need the words, love, joy, or delight when you experience beautiful music to be moved by the music.

The mind is just the mind. A pile of thoughts and concepts. We are used to identifying with this mind and so we have a hard time imagining anything else. But the sooner you can pull away from being dependant on concepts, you will experience a free world of existence-being that is beautiful and wholesome without having to conceptualize beauty or wholeness. You have experienced it before, and the next time you do, and you are alert, you will remember all the other times you experienced the beauty of freedom from concepts as well.

While you contemplate the above passage until you fully understand it, consider the following information to help you work with the reality in which you find yourself.

You can change the way you interact with reality to get positive results. The following points below will assist in this regard.

1. Lighten up.

2. Don't take yourself so seriously.

3. Let go of your attachment to how you think things should be.

4. Pay attention to the way things are, and make peace with that.

Once you can do those four things, you are in an open and free space to make choices.

By "Lighten Up" I mean to quit making everything so heavy and important. (Within reason of course). Pulling from the examples above: If your spouse doesn't like your parents, so what? Do you and your spouse get along and love each other? If so, great. If not, then deal with that and don't project that prime problem on a peripheral problem.

Did you get angry the other day, when someone insulted you? So what? That's normal. Now if you continue to dwell, then that's a problem, and might get in the way of your spiritual progress. Why? Because you become what you dwell on. Dwell on the divine, not anger. Yet if anger arises, let it pass like a cloud before the sun.

Do you consider yourself a spiritual person, but still really enjoy sex? Well, you are a spiritual being having a human experience. If your sex life doesn't border on perversion, it's not going to get in the way of your progress. So have fun!

By "Don't Take Your Self So Seriously", I mean that in the overall scheme of things you are not really that important. After you're dead, no one is really going to think about you all that much. And that's good, because you will have moved on to another plane, and you don't need to think about them either, because you've got other things to do!

Does the thought bother you that you aren't that important? If so, you've got some things to work on. Lahiri Mahasaya, a great spiritual teacher, once said, "I am nothing and no one." He went on to express by holding that idea, one can quickly reach liberation.

Just because you are nothing important, doesn't mean there isn't a work of the divine consciousness coming through. You are not important, but the expression of the divine is the only thing that is important.

By "Let Go of Your Attachment to How You Think Things Should Be", I am continuing the theme, that you need to pay attention to what is in reality, and not how you expect things to go. Often, they will go your way. And as you get clearer, through your meditation, they will most definitely go your way more often. Not because you are willing something to occur, but because you are clear and receptive and so the ideas that are generated in your mind are more divinely inspired and in line with the natural trends of life.

By "Pay Attention to the Way Things Are and Make Peace With That" I am implying that your judgment about the goodness or badness of a situation doesn't really help matters. If something is occurring and you can't get out of the situation or don't know an immediate way to change it, be still. Be at peace. Let it pass, or wait for an inspiration that will help solve the dilemma. But make sure that as you are experiencing the situation, you are at peace. Judgment, anxiety, and denying reality only muck up the divine radio signal that's coming your way.

Remember, this all really boils down to accepting consequences. If you want to be enlightened and 90% of the enlightenment teachers in the world say it's valuable to meditate to experience that, then you need to weigh the consequences of either meditating regularly or not. If you want to live a healthy long life, and 90% of the people who are educated in this realm recommend regular exercise, a nutritious diet, and a stress management program, then you need to weigh the consequences of either following or not following this advice. Whatever you decide on, accept the possible consequences, and then move on.

What ever you do in life, don't linger. No circumstances can ever be repeated. The river of the dead looks back to the past and holds to what could have or should have been. The river of life moves ever onward. Merge with the river of life.

CHAPTER 8

PRACTICING YOUR FAITH

*That one who has faith has God-knowledge.
For the doubting person, neither in this world
nor the realms beyond, is there happiness.*
              - Bhagavad Gita 4: 39,40

We are practicing our faith at every moment. That which we hold to be true about life and its processes manifests, because it is the nature of consciousness to reflect what is presented to it. However we expect life to be, will be brought into our life experience either in the near or distant future. There are, at least, three levels of influence on our consciousness that shapes our life experience and determines our faith: our conscious thoughts, our subconscious storehouse of memories and past thoughts, and the thoughts and ideas of other people. To be a spiritual master, a fully mature human being, entails gaining dominion over what we allow to shape our faith.

Our minds are built of past perceptions. The building plans that create structure out of our past perceptions is based on our judgments. As we make judgments on experiences, we sow the seeds of our future. We arrange those past perceptions in a certain way, based on the direction of our judgment. As has always been true, what you sow is what you reap.

Imagine you are attempting to master a musical instrument, and during your early months of first getting acquainted with the notes of the scale, where to put your fingers, and how to hold the instrument you meet with failure at every turn. You play your scales wrong. You have a hard time following the metronome. You get a kink in your neck, because you have poor posture. Now, let's look at two different possible perspectives in relation to these events.

Option 1 Thought Process: "This is terrible! I hate this instrument! I'm not any good at all. My friends were right, and I should stop wasting my time learning to make beautiful music!"

Option 2 Thought Process: "Hmmm. This is turning out to be harder than I thought. I guess I'm going to have to slow down and focus on one aspect of this at a time. That's OK. All this hard work is going to pay off, when I can finally play that song I love so much. Let's get back to work!"

Note that the experience, or the reality of the experience, was exactly the same from both of these perspectives. The difference came in the interpretation of the experience. From those interpretations, the person who chose thought process number one, gave up on music and eventually took a job that was boring and tedious. Every time she listened to the music she loved, she thought back with regret on letting a few obstacles (ones that nearly every musician goes through) get in the way. The person who chose thought process number two, went on to play in a symphony and became a teacher, inspiring young children to also express their own music through their chosen instrument. She's happy for the most part, and looks forward to her work in music everyday. This same principle is applicable to our spiritual growth process.

It is easy to think that anyone with spiritual clarity and peace made no effort to this end. When we think this way, we can make excuses such as:

"There is something special about that person that I'll never have, at least not in this life time."

"They had better opportunities and better information."

"I'm not as strong as them or as dedicated."

"They can just close their eyes and meditate without any distraction or thought."

"It was easy for them to think positively and have faith in the process."

Again, we must remember that these are all excuses. For a person to experience success in anything, it requires a strong faith and dedication to maintain the course until the desired end is reached. This is applicable to music, building a business, having money, being a nice person, and even enlightenment.

Now, I'm certain that our life is infinite and that the body, mind and personality are the only things that really change. I'm also sure that as we move from one body to the other we carry our states of consciousness with us. The personality may be a little different, and the history will change with each incarnation, but deep down inside, whatever state of consciousness we had in our last incarnation is most certainly going to show up again once our mind, body, nervous system and personality come to full maturity this time around.

This being the case, you can bet that any spiritually aware person had to wrestle with impatience, greed, lust, the monkey mind, lack of faith, disease, mental instability, being honest, developing a sense of unyielding happiness for no reason, etc, either earlier on in this lifetime or at some other point in infinity before they expressed soul consciousness as clearly as they do now.

To think otherwise is just creating another false story that will empower your own lack of clarity about what you really have to do if you want to wake up. They did it. You can too. You can say you are too old or too young or too wild or two worldly. It doesn't matter where you are on the circle of infinity, you can find an excuse. When you decide to stop making excuses and start getting down to business, you will begin moving forward in the direction you want to go.

If you choose to doubt this perspective, you will experience situations that sustain your doubt. If you choose to adopt this perspective, you will find that with hard work and renewed enthusiasm, a new and life-affirming paradigm will dawn in your awareness.

Three Levels of Influence

As mentioned above, our faith is determined by the current thinking processes we are aware of, the accumulation of past thoughts in the subconscious, and the thoughts of others. All of these need to be dealt with to reshape our faith. Being realistic, this can be quite a job. But remember, we are infinite beings. We have as long as it takes to accomplish this end. Wasting your time without undertaking this task is only prolonging your experience in infinity as being negative and less than enjoyable.

Our current thinking process is the most immediate level of influence we can change. These are most specifically related to our judgments about reality. If you find that you are thinking negatively about anything, the immediate response is to admit you have had this habit in the past, but to choose to think positively now. What ever reason you have to think negatively is just your excuse, with no correspondence to reality. Countless people have experienced terrible atrocities, and yet still remain buoyant and optimistic. Countless people also have everything handed to them on a silver platter, and can still find reasons to complain. It's up to you to decide which way you go in life.

At the outset, this may feel like a waste of time. Your negativity persists. You feel you are lying to yourself about the possible positive potential of an outcome. You may even begin to experience a quick result of your change of thinking. Something that was about to turn out bad, may unexpectedly turn out good. Then, like clockwork, you think, "But this isn't going to last. When is the other shoe going to drop?" Then things go wrong, and you say, "See? I knew that was going to happen!" **This is faith in action**.

But if you persist, doing your best to change one little thought at a time, eventually those little drops of thought accumulate into a bucket full of positive faith. Continue, and eventually you have a garden filled with positive thoughts ready to germinate and sprout. The quickness with which you fill your mind with positive expectations is in relation to your receptivity and stubbornness. If you say, "I'm too stubborn to change too quickly." Watch your thoughts. Reaffirm, "I am done with the habit of stubbornness and can accept quick results of my change of thinking." Keep this up until your acceptance of good fortune is more powerful than your past habit of accepting ill fortune. **Whichever has the most gravity within you wins, and** *a habits particular gravity grows with the more attention and intention we invest in it.*

Our subconscious, which stimulates our deep feeling state, is vast indeed. You can do your best to change your thinking, but if your subconscious does not align with that thinking, you are at odds with your self, and potentially canceling out your intentions. If you say, "I am very willing to do what it takes to be spiritually free," yet, in the pit of your stomach, you feel, "Well, yes, this is true, but only if I don't really have to challenge my current way of life. As long as I don't have to make any major changes, then yes, I am willing to do what it takes to be spiritually free." This is one certain way to not experience spiritual freedom, because you are not one hundred percent committed.

You may say, "I'd like to make more money." Or "I'd like to have perfect health." Yet, when someone offers you work, your inner feelings come up as a sense of resistance, and your actions will show your inner subconscious beliefs. You will be late for your interview, or forget to set your alarm, or just decide the work is too hard and say to yourself, "Well, that's just not the right job for me." When you decide to have perfect health, it may be easy to tell yourself, "I'm healthy and happy!" Yet you may find that your subconscious does not agree, because you take no initiative to exercise or to get enough rest, or to choose to avoid actions which inevitably cause suffering.

Watch your actions and your inner gut reactions to any changes you make in your conscious thinking process. If your actions do not align with the new way of thinking, you may need to work on your subconscious too. One very helpful method is to set up your life so that you can ignore your thinking mind while changing your subconscious and thereby strengthening your faith. Here is an exercise to help you get around the inertia of the subconscious.

Exercise to Change the Subconscious

Example 1: You decide that you want to be more spiritually awake. You've changed your thinking process, so you are no longer telling your self the story that it is too hard and you don't deserve it, or that you are too young or too old. You read spiritual inspirational literature every night before sleep and do your best to eat your vegetables, exercise, pay your bills, and be friendly. Yet, every morning your alarm goes off at 6 AM, the time you decided to meditate. Your thoughts kick in and say, "But it's so comfortable here. I need all of my rest for work, so I can do a good job." Then you unplug the alarm, and drift back into sleep.

Proper response: The night before, as you fall asleep, you tell your self, "I am going to get up at 6 AM, and meditate. Before I even begin thinking I'm going to get out of bed and go sit in my meditation chair."

The alarm goes off at 6 AM. Before your mind gets a chance to engage, you swing your feet out of bed. Put on your robe, and go sit down in your meditation chair and begin with a short prayer, then you practice your chosen meditation technique.

You do this every day. The mind doesn't get a chance to engage and express all your subconscious conditioning and resistance towards meditation. Before the mind knows what is happening, you are already sitting and meditating. You then find your mind was wrong and that you actually have more energy and are more peaceful by starting your day on such a positive decisive note. If you can do that, you can be successful in just about any other undertaking.

Example 2: You have always wanted to write a book. You have many great ideas, enjoy reading, and have always wanted to contribute your own creativity to the world. Yet, you have made up a reality that you need to be an English major, and you need more time, and you aren't that creative anyway. You tell yourself it is a pipe dream, etc. The result of this kind of faith is that you spend your evenings watching TV, and waste time on the internet surfing for information that has no bearing on your life.

The alternative is that you decide you are not going to tell yourself that story anymore. Every day you wake up and say "I'm ready to write that book! As soon as I get home from work, I'm going to get started." You get home from work, think about your book, and then get sidetracked on the internet or doing laundry, or staring out the window. Your subconscious resistance is at work.

The solution is that you tell yourself, "I am going to write that book and I'm going to do it every day after work for at least 30 minutes to an hour." Now, as soon as you get home, before the kids favorite TV show is over, and they are demanding your attention, you immediately sit down at your computer and start typing. You brainstorm. You type whatever comes in regards to your ideas about the book. It doesn't even matter if you don't know what you are doing. The point is that you get started and you don't give your mind a chance to engage in all its subconscious falsity about the impossibility of this project. A half hour goes by and now you are excited. You don't want to stop. You experience the success of starting, so that every day when you get home, you don't think about your negative faith in your abilities. You immediately sit down and start writing.

You may find that you do need more information about how to write dialogue or sculpt a plot or make believable characters, but now you are no longer surfing the internet mindlessly. You are looking for books on writing books. You are reading forums about the best way to publish. As the months and years go by, your thirty minutes to one hour a day, turns into a passion, and you have a completed novel.

This same process can be applied to any area of life. Set a specific time each day to take action in your chosen endeavor. Don't think about your chosen endeavor through out the day. Then when the bell rings indicating it is time to take action, you immediately start doing whatever it is you have chosen. *You circumvent the mind and your subconscious and begin reshaping your subconscious, your faith and your destiny to a new end.*

Your Task

Pick something you have always wanted to do. Set aside a realistic and specific amount of time every day, at the same time every day, that you are going to dedicate to accomplishing your chosen endavor. Set an alarm if you have to. Don't go through your day anticipating this event, because that gives your subconscious plenty of time to fill your conscious mind with reasons as to why this is silly. Just decide that you are going to do it, and no thoughts or doubts or anything or anyone is going to get in the way. Once the alarm goes off, you will know it's time to begin. Immediately go to where you can get to work and start the process.

It doesn't matter if this is a "spiritual" goal or a normal everyday goal. Once you can master this process with one aspect of your life it will be applicable to any aspect. I have also found, that my spiritual growth and inner poise has increased simply by being more purposeful and finding that I can do what I say I'm going to do. I meditate better and am happier throughout the day. You are learning to reshape your subconscious, and as your successes or at least your tenacity to succeed continues, resistance to success falls away, until your natural state is a successful one.

Other People

Other people have been shaping our lives, by our own concession, for as long as we've been alive. In an ideal world, we would be raised by healthy-minded parents and family, surrounded by supportive friends and coworkers. You may have noticed that for many people, this is not the case.

The way we see the world, what we expect, our judgment and ultimately our faith, is usually in direct relation to the people around us. Luckily, after we grow up and move out we have the capacity to assess the validity of the faith we have accepted from other people and decide if it is useful, or if we need to recreate a faith that is more useful to our purposes in this world. Just as we may seek out a church that is more in line with our spiritual faith, we can seek out new people that are in line with our life faith.

Listen to the messages you are given by those around you. Are they positive and encouraging? Are the messages demeaning, and restrictive? Do they say, "Sure you can accomplish those little things, but don't get too ambitious!" Why not be ambitious? Think of the messages you were given as a child. Are they still valid? Do you find it worthwhile to keep listening to them? Do you think that the people who gave you those messages are special in some way, or entitled to a specific revelation of truth that you are not? Look at the quality of the lives of the people whose messages you allow into your consciousness. Are they happy, successful, wise, and good to the world? If so, their messages may be worth considering. If not, consider if you like participating in their faith, and make a decision.

We are eternal beings, temporarily identifying with a personality, history, mind and body. There is no merit in maintaining a state of consciousness that is no longer useful to you. Change is constant in the external world. Our faith in life can change too and it should, otherwise we become living fossils of a lost age. When we are children we may see God as a child does. As we mature, so does our understanding about life. Wear your faith like a garment. When that garment becomes old, worn and useless, cast it off, and decide to take up the mantle of a faith that more accurately reflects your aspirations. As you stay true to your path in life, you will know when a change of direction is called for. Have faith in the universe to provide what you need when you need it, and you will experience the endless flow of grace that is accessible to anyone who chooses to accept it.

Faith is the essence of how our life expresses in this world. The Gita states that, "one who does not have faith or is of a doubting nature perishes." This is because if we have no faith or aspiration we are in decay. To doubt is to negate. That which you doubt has little power if any tangible force in your life experience. Joseph Campbell said, "You see no Gods outside of you, because there are none within you." If you have faith in a divine presence, or your higher Self, that aspect of consciousness is empowered and you can depend on it.

Faith the size of a mustard seed, is said to have the power to move a mountain. The best medicine in the world can fail if we do not believe in its efficacy. Similarly, in Yogananda's *Autobiography of a Yogi*, friend of the great Sri Yutkeswar was healed from a fatal experience by seven drops of lamp oil because of the powerful force behind Lahiri Mahasaya's faith.

William Blake once wrote, "If the Sun and the Moon should doubt, they'd immediately go out." He also wrote, "The questioner who sits so sly, shall never know how to reply, he who replies to words of doubt, doth put the light of knowledge out." We can confuse wisdom and knowledge with the thinking mind, but that does not make our thoughts knowledge. Knowledge, real knowledge comes from within. It is an inner knowing, and cannot be explained in words. By your meditation practice and surrender of your limited ego to a higher power, you tap into soul liberating knowledge. You no longer have to convert people to prove your view point is correct. You no longer have to explain to others why you believe what you do, because it is enough that you know it.

To have faith is not to hope something will occur or that something is true. Hope implies doubt. Faith is the power of life. Remember, if the sun or moon doubted they would promptly go out. To have faith is to live.

It is good to remember, that one faith is not better than another, just as meditation techniques or spiritual teachers are not in competition. No matter the chosen expression of our faith, if we stay true to our path, we will experience the results of our commitment. Then we will know happiness, because we will have followed our calling to the very end, and then we can return from the journey and tell others what we have seen and experienced. We can strengthen the faith of our fellow travelers, and sustain the divine expression of life.

One Last Thought

This can be a lot to take in all at once. There can be many changes that you can imagine need to occur to be successful in reshaping your faith and moving into a state of spiritual tranquility. To say to your self, "OK, from now on I am always going to have faith, and be purposeful and always make the right decision, from now until the end of my life" is a good way to overload your system and then promptly give up, when on day three you slip back into old patterns. ***The best way to approach this transformational process is one day at a time.***

Spend some time reflecting on what your life of faith would look like when all is said and done. What will you have accomplished? How will you have lived? What values and ideals will you have chosen to express? What will people say about you after you are no longer in their presence? Write these down. After you've taken some time to get clear on this, then decide that for the rest of the day, you are going to do your best to live in such a way as to support these intentions. However, unnatural it may feel, you are going to get used to it until it becomes enjoyable and pleasant.

You'll wake up tomorrow and promptly decide you are going to do your best to live up to this new idea of your self. Then through your own will power, and divine grace, you will take the steps towards that end.

There will be moments, hours or even days, that you fall off the path you've decided to walk, and get a little turned around. As soon as you are aware of this, you decide you are going to find that path and start walking again. No guilt. No shame. No beating yourself up. When you fall down, get up. As long as you are gentle with yourself and persistent in your new vision, your new faith will eventually grow up out of the dirt and reach to the sun, where it will finally blossom, sharing its fragrance with the world.

CHAPTER 9

FORGIVENESS

According to the dictionary, the definition of forgiveness is, "to cease to blame or hold resentment against." Resentment and the inability to forgive is a major obstacle to spiritual realization on multiple levels. It locks us in a pattern of anger, or despair. It bathes our bodies in stress hormones that tear down our immune system, damage our genetics, destroy our brain cells, and create conditions for heart disease. By not learning the proper way to forgive, we hold our attention on a pattern of negativity, and continue to define our self as a limited being, a victim of circumstance. To what noble end, do we do this? For what reason, do we torture ourselves?

Life on earth is precious. Here we have bodies that span the material, astral, causal and transcendent realms. On this world we have the marvelous capacity to neutralize karmas that span the breadth of our existence. To waste our lives in an energy pattern of accusation and spite, serves only to deplete our vitality, and wastes our life that could be better utilized in cleaning up our karma and strengthening the experience of love and harmony within our being.

It's been said that the greatest obstacle to tranquility and spiritual realization is sustaining a false sense of self. We do this by identifying with our bodies, minds, history and personality. We do this by maintaining an inflated sense of self importance, meaning that there is something special about our specific incarnation. When we do this, we are affirming that we are separate from the wholeness of life. We hold on to feelings of low self-esteem, affirming that there, again, is something so special about us, that we are to be mistreated and fail at everything we do. Both of these states result in a sense of separation. To maintain a sense that you have been wronged, victimized, and mistreated, and to hold on to those feelings is a way of telling the universe that you don't want to take responsibility for your states of consciousness and experiences in life. You are blaming a world "out there" for what happened to you.

Now it may be that you have been mistreated, or even injured and severely traumatized by another person or situation. And while you always have a choice, you may not have consciously known that at the time, and so the negative event occurred. As we grow in wisdom, we learn that no matter what happens to us, we can choose how we want to respond to that situation. We can say, "That terrible thing happened to me! I cannot forgive the other person for what they did to me!" And there is the potential that what we are really saying is, "I hated that situation. I am angry at my self for letting life move in such a way, that I allowed that to occur! I cannot forgive myself for my own choices that led to that situation."

Bad things happen to good people. Good things happen to bad people. There is seemingly no sense to it. But if you look beyond the immediate, external conditions of this life, we can consider that we have been embodied countless times. Even in this lifetime, we have played countless roles. Sometimes we have been angelic and kind. Other times we have been angry and conceited and vicious. Sometimes our thoughts are pure and wholesome and loving. At other times, our thoughts are dark and malevolent. All of these thoughts, actions and chosen roles add up. There is a mixture of good and bad. Knowing that, we can see that there will be times when good seeds sprout up easily, and a time when thorny weeds of karma will sprout up in our garden.

To be tranquil is to make peace with the fact that we have been haphazardly tending our garden without much of a plan or forethought. To this end, the seeds that sprout are a combination of positive and negative experiences. They grow based on the appropriate season, weather conditions, and environment. Once we accept this, we can begin the process of analyzing our inner and outer circumstances to get an idea of what is really deep down below our conscious mind (the dirt) and pay attention to what we are really growing.

We begin by being mindful in our daily life. We see our thoughts of anger sprout up and we decide to pluck them out of the dirt and no longer water those thoughts. We see ourselves as the victims of bad habits. We note this, and decide, that's enough of that. Each time a bad habit arises we cut it down, and pull up the roots by no longer indulging in the habit. Each time a new shoot of negative habit pops through the earth, we grab it and throw it out. We watch our circumstances around us, and with dispassion we see the people in our lives and how they affect us. Those that make us feel bad and do not sustain our spirit peace, we remove from our garden, one by one. The thoughts and situations that give rise to violence against our bodies and mind are also to be weeded out.

We notice that good plants come up as well. The roses of friendship grow. The delicious apple trees of kindness and love, poke up through the dirt. The nectarine plant of financial good fortune force up through the weeds. Thoughts of discipline and service, struggle towards the sunshine. Feelings of joy and divine wholeness are hidden and scrawny beneath the vines of envy and vice. In our mindfulness, we clear away the obstacles to the growth of these divine aspects of our nature. We let these karmas grow until they bloom and are pollinated by the bee of optimism. Then when they go to seed, we purposefully plant more. We continue to weed out that which drags our souls through the mud, and plant those wondrous seeds that lift us into divine peace.

The key is to do this with dispassion, the state or quality of being unemotional or emotionally uninvolved. By that, I mean that we do not freak out by all the weeds that we have in the garden, or all the work that it is going to take to clean it up. We see the job, we do the job, and we let the end result be what it will be. We do not stress over how few seeds of joy we have. We collect the seeds that we can, and day by day, we plant more. For each choice we make to be joyful and to avoid harmful circumstances and people, we are blessed with a new handful of beautiful seeds. All of this can take time, but the other option is to remain in your weed overgrown garden of negativity, limitation and restriction. Who knows, maybe the first weed that needs to be singled out is the weed of laziness and apathy? Make a priority list, and start with one negative tendency at a time. Eventually, you will find the list is empty, and now all you have to do is tend your flowers.

Note on letting go of past situations that were unpleasant: No matter who or what did something bad to you, you can decide to do your best to not allow that situation to happen again. You were receptive to the situation for whatever reason. You don't need to find out why, you need to decide to not make choices that lead back to that experience. You can decide that by the grace of God or the cosmic power within you, you are no longer receptive to that situation. The more you affirm that, you will find that you often make choices that do not lead down the dark road of your past. So you see, there is no reason to blame anyone or anything for what happened to you, because the past cannot be changed anyway. But you can reclaim your divine right to choose and make sure that you are willing to avoid such circumstances in the future.

Our Ancestral Influences

When we were children and developing our sense of self, we took pride in being somebody. It was a joyous time of coming into manifestation, building up a personality, and exploring our talents and interests. The seeds of our past karmas were beginning to sprout in the Spring of life. Yet, many of us found that our personality was being incubated in an unsupportive environment. Rather than the roses of love and grace, it was the weeds of egotism and self-centeredness that were cultivated.

For every success, we were met with expectations that were unreasonable. We heard our caretakers criticizing us, or reacting to our curiosity out of fear. We watched our parents, take pride in the negative side of life. "Can you believe what that person did to me," they would say, thereby demonstrating that our ego, and our sense of importance was based on the imagined insolence of other people. As time went by, we also began to adopt this method of defining our sense of self.

Suffering from resentment, requires the following equation:

> (A lack of responsibility for the circumstances in which we find our selves) + (An inflated sense of importance) − (The wisdom that the world presents to us what we present to it) = (The need for forgiveness)

Variable 1 – A lack of responsibility and how to address it

When I was younger, I had this weird idea. When I would hear about a person's problems or difficult circumstances, I found myself often thinking, and to the displeasure of those around me saying out loud, "Well, they must enjoy it. Otherwise, why would they continue to experience it?" Now, that seemed a little odd coming out of the mouth of a kid in junior high school. And it was comments like that, that consistently prompted my grandmother to say I needed an attitude adjustment. However, it's now twenty some years later, and I am still sticking by that assertion.

Now, at the time, that comment was coming from my feeling that if something was unpleasant, I was going to do whatever it took to get away from that unpleasantness. And I couldn't understand why others didn't follow that same logic. That makes sense to just about anyone, right? However, as the years went by I started to notice that I possessed a strange aberration that was great for spiritual growth but not so accepted by the majority of society. This was a certain lack of attachment.

As we grow up we are surrounded by people. These are family, friends, etc. Our minds get used to their familiarity. We let down our guard and feel safe, even if their company isn't really that supportive. We are lulled into a trance-like state. Even if the people around us, belittle us, support negative habits, perpetuate moods, or prevent us from attaining our highest goals, we don't mind, because we are comfortable. This is not really a problem unless you deny the truth of the situation.

What do I mean by "deny the truth of the situation"? Well, if you are where you are in life, and you are saying things like:

"I can't ever be happy."

"It's impossible to get healthy."

"The world is an unsafe place."

"Who do I think I am, thinking I can know the reality of God."

"I'll never find a relationship where I am loved and respected."

"There is no basis to the assertion that we live in a supportive universe."

And let's imagine that you say, "I can't ever be happy," because you subject yourself to friends that wallow in their grief, talk about one depressing life episode after another, etc, yet you make no effort to tell them to be quiet or find new friends...

Or that you say, "It's impossible to get healthy," because everyone you socialize with either watches TV, drinks too much, smokes too much, and never once has the idea to go exercise or play an active sport...

Or you say, "The world is an unsafe place," because you are attached to people that gossip about the latest terror attack or shooting in a city 500 miles away, and don't have any motivation to lift yourself out of that kind of company…

Maybe you say, "Who do I think I am, thinking I can know the reality of God?" Or "There is no basis to the assertion that we live in a supportive universe," because everyone around you is too focused on their human frailties, rather than accepting a higher possibility, and you just love them all so much, you can't bear to find company that is less stuck in that mode of thinking…

Or maybe you say, "I'll never find a relationship where I am loved and respected" and you come home every night to a partner who belittles you and insults you in front of the kids, or criticizes your dreams, yet you made a commitment to them 8 years ago, and by God you are going to see that commitment to the end…

These are all direct examples of denying the truth of a situation. The real truth is that you are attached to circumstances that don't support you, and you don't have the motivation to make a change. This is understandable. 99% of the planet lives like this. So it's not really a problem, unless you truly do want to be happy, tranquil and spiritually aware.

Sounds a little harsh, yet it is the way it works.

Jesus said, "Whoever comes to me and does not give up father and mother, wife and children, brothers and sisters, yes, and even life itself, cannot be my disciple." (Luke 14:26) "None of you can become my disciple if you do not give up all your possessions." (Luke 14:32)

At the initiation into a spiritual tradition, an initiate is asked to bring a fruit, a flower and a modest donation. The fruit is to represent giving up the fruits of our actions. The flower represents our devotion to the path. The monetary donation represents putting all of our resources at the service of the path. This is not to make the spiritual organization rich, but to symbolically indicate that we are willing to give up everything for that which we seek, remembrance of our oneness in divinity.

Lahiri Mahasaya was known to have asked a disciple before initiation if the disciple would give Lahiri all of his money, his possessions, his family and his wife. Now Lahiri didn't want these things for himself. He was asking only to find out the extent of the disciple's sincerity.

In a story from Autobiography of a Yogi, a man had scaled the Himalayas in search of the master Babaji. When he finally came to Babaji's camp he asked to be Babaji's disciple. Babaji refused and the man threatened to throw himself over the edge of the cliff if he was not accepted. Babaji said, "Then jump." The man tossed himself off the cliff, killing himself. Babaji, asked his disciples to go get the man and bring his body back. Babaji brought the man back to life, and then accepted him as a disciple.

As you can see, in all of these situations, we must be honest about our intentions. If we want to go all the way, then we do what is necessary. We give up our attachments and move forward. If we don't, we need to be honest and say, "Yes, I'll do a little, but I am happy in this normal human state. Don't expect too much of me and I won't either."

If you can be firm in your decision to go all the way, or be honest about what you are willing to do, you won't have to put your self through mental or psychological agony, because you are being self honest about what you will and will not do, and that you are willing to accept the consequences.

What does this have to do with forgiveness? Let me get through a description of the other variables, and then we'll tie it all together.

Variable 2 – An inflated sense of self-importance

By thinking that you are so special, that people mistreated you, just because they "had it in for you" specifically, is a great way to keep on inflated sense of self importance. If you think that way, then you are going to find reasons in your environment and in the people around you to continue to generate situations that support that notion. Believe it or not, most people mistreat other people because they are unclear about the meaning of their own lives. They do not yet understand or remember that what they do to another person they are doing to God and their very selves. They have been hypnotized to think that if they can do something to dominate or injure another, they will know true power. They are misguided, partially because they were not shown another way in this world. If you accept their authority and allow them to scar you for life, you are supporting their own inflated sense of self importance. You continue the problem and prevent the world from waking up. You sustain your own inflated sense of self importance as a victim, and sustain their sense of self importance as the perpetrator. Why do you think Jesus said:

"You have heard that it was said, 'An eye for an eye, and a tooth for a tooth.' But I tell you, do not resist an evil person. If someone strikes you on the right cheek, turn to him the other also. And if someone wants to sue you and take your tunic, let him have your cloak as well. If someone forces you to go one mile, go with him two miles. Give to the one who asks you, and do not turn away from the one who wants to borrow from you."

He said it because this neutralizes the false sense of self and separateness of all parties involved. This is the work that we are working towards, not our own tranquility and love, but a universal tranquility and love. If no one else showed the perpetrators in your life how to love and be kind, then it is your job.

Now obviously, this doesn't mean to seek out situations where this will occur. But if they have already occurred, or are currently occurring, you can love and bless those around you, then move on and choose different circumstances. The inflated sense of self importance is then neutralized, because you no longer invest your precious divine life on this earth in feelings of resentment, anger or revenge.

Oh, and by the way, in the situation you feel you need to forgive, it's pretty safe to say, that even if you weren't there to be on the receiving end, someone else would've been. People who like to harm others, have a way of finding receptive outlets and it doesn't seem to matter very much who it is.

Variable 3 – The World Gives Us What We Give It

One of the prime mistakes spiritual aspirants make in this life is that they think if they meditate and pray daily, yet do not tend their mental and emotional garden, that everything works out just fine. They then wonder why life doesn't improve very much, or at least as much as it has for the spiritual masters they look up to. We've already discussed the garden metaphor, but it is worth revisiting.

As you go through your day, you need to pay attention to the thoughts that go through your head, and the emotions you habitually feel. As you fall asleep at night, watch the thoughts that go through your mind. They are a clear indicator of what station your dial is turned to, and what you can expect your life ahead to be like.

After you notice the habitual thoughts you think, feelings you feel and expectations and beliefs about life, you need to make a conscious effort to choose new thoughts and feelings and expectations. Does this take vigilance and work? Yes, it does. Is some savior going to come out of the sky or appear in a vision to do this for you? No. All truthful spiritual teachers admit that they are there to point a seeker in the proper direction or to be a good example, yet they are not there to do the work for the student.

A good health coach, can empower you with positive thoughts and push you to see just what you are really capable of, but they can't force you to eat healthy food or lift heavy weights. You have to do that yourself. The company of supportive people carries you a long way, but for lasting results you have to do the work yourself, so then you can move into that role of being the support for others. By admitting that there are supportive people in the world and that you are one of them, you attract supportive people.

You Don't Need Forgiveness

If you affirm that you need to be more forgiving or that you need to develop forgiveness, what you are saying to the Universe is: "Hello Universe, would you please send me some reasons that will empower my decision that I have to work on being more forgiving?"

What you need, is to admit that you have more control over your life situation than you let on. What you need to say:

"I've made some choices, that one way or the other led me to experience these negative circumstances. Maybe I know what those

choices are and maybe I don't. And if I don't, I'm just going to say 'it must be a past life karma'. But whatever the reason, I'm done with it. I am going to do my utmost best to avoid thoughts, feelings, people and places that rekindle my desire to put myself in a difficult situation.

"If I screw up every now and again, fine. I'm still not going to blame the other person. I'm going to reassess what I could have done differently, and do it.

"If there is nothing I can do, I'm going to be thankful that at least I was here to bear the brunt of this situation so someone else didn't Then I'm going to give it up to God, so no one else has to hear about or deal with it."

Note: If you need counseling to deal with a situation, there is nothing wrong with that. Just don't turn the need for counseling into a hobby."

Love

Once you have this under control, then you need to practice love. Love transforms all that it touches. In a state of love, there is safety and peace, and an openness to change. Why do you think Gandhi chose the path of non-violence? It was through transforming violence with love, that the world was changed.

Aggression, difficulty, anger, violence, perversity and jealousy are all manifestations of a frustrated life. When there is no outlet or no sense of possibility of being heard, understood or loved, these negative expressions of God manifest. In a state of love, all is accepted and heard. The energy of the negative expression unwinds its self. Every time negativity is met by love, the unwinding continues. One day, there will be nothing left to unwind. We will know our blissful tranquil state, all of us will. But in the meantime, we have to create that state within ourselves. For every person that undertakes this task, it becomes easier for the current and future generations to open up to the possibility of love and being.

Of course, remember, that love can take many manifestations. We are not talking about "idiot love", or being someone's door mat. Wisdom is strong and decisive, while also being surrendered and compassionate. You can love another person, yet be clear that you don't take any negativity from them. That is love, because it shows strength, and it also shows love for the individualized self (you) which is equally an expression of the divine. Some times you have to tell another person to "knock it off" or you need to restrain them from violence, or give them an ultimatum. As long as it is done without attachment, smugness or enjoyment, then it is still love.

CHAPTER 10

KNOWING THE TRUTH OF UNITY CONSCIOUSNESS

Because you are in variety, you say you understand unity -- that you have flashes, etc., remember things, etc.; you consider this variety to be real. On the other hand Unity is the reality, and the variety is false. The variety must go before unity reveals itself -- its reality. It is always real. It does not send flashes of its being in this false variety. On the contrary, this variety obstructs the truth.
-Ramana Maharshi

The past chapters are meant to serve as a proper foundation to launch this process of moving into tranquility. As it is stated in the Gita, "First, we are to work to discover what we are, and become Self-realized. Once we know what we are, then our work is to remain in tranquility."

Once we set in motion the principles outlined in the previous chapters, we are to continue tending our garden and let the seeds of our positive intention to learn and grow come to fruition. As this continues, we then have our capacities directed to understanding what we are, and to experience the truth of life and its meaning.

Since this work is not intended to birth a religion or a new dogma, you may find that you still need a religious observance, or a specific teaching to guide your quest for self-knowledge and tranquility. By all means, explore your Bible, Gita, Yoga Sutras, Buddhist texts, Koran, Zen, etc. The morality and lifestyle regimens will do well to keep your days organized and focused, which is useful for everyone. Let the words of the following chapters guide your mind into contemplation and direct experience of reality "as it is" and acceptance of full knowledge of what you are beyond your false sense of self.

Now we move into the deeper side of practice. In the second half of these lessons, we will challenge the most instinctual and ingrained tendencies a human being can cling to. It is these final threads we endeavor to clip, that we may float free into our pure conscious nature, while living out a natural life in this realm, or in any realm we may find to inhabit.

The quote from Ramana Maharshi, at the top of this chapter, summarizes one of the prime difficulties a spiritual aspirant faces as they move more fully into their pure conscious, tranquil nature -- the false idea that we exist as separate and varied beings, and are trying to re-experience our unity with the wholeness of life.

The devotee says, "I am experiencing separateness from God and the divine consciousness. I want to know Unity consciousness. I want to know my pure blissful nature. When I meditate I have flashes of insight into oneness and peace, but then I re-experience this sense of separateness."

The Great Sage responds, "Unity consciousness does not send flashes of its being into this false variety. The Unity is always there, the reality. Yet the waves of our concept of variety washes over it, and so we only see the Unity, when the waves recede.

"It is the concept of variety and separateness that obstructs the truth of unity. When we can see through the concept of variety, unity will reveal itself clearly."

Keep in mind, this is only my conjecture of how this conversation could be stretched out. But the point of all this, is that, typically we say we are separate from the divine infinite consciousness, and on those days when we have a really great meditation or an extremely satisfying stress free day, that we catch a glimpse of unity consciousness and peace. When we say we are longing for unity, we are affirming a duality and separateness.

Unity, duality, separateness, these are all just words. They have no corresponding reality. Envision what would happen if you dropped these concepts. If there is no Unity, then there is no duality. If there is no longing to be reunited in God, then there is no separateness from God. It is the words and concepts we use that keep us from experiencing reality, as it is, right now.

Exercise - *Accept The Reality of Unity Now*

Step 1 –When you next meditate, avoid any thoughts that you are doing this to become closer to God or your Self. Of course the thoughts will arise. Just ignore them. A good friend once told me, "Just because someone tells you something, doesn't mean you have to believe it." The same goes for your thoughts. Just because they show you possibilities and ideas, doesn't mean you have to listen to them or even buy their product.

Step 2 – Use your meditation technique, because you know it is going to calm your mind and emotions and settle down the waves that make you think and feel you are separate from the wholeness of life. Do this until you are settled and peaceful. Then simply sit. Acknowledging that the room you are inhabiting, the couch you are sitting on, the candle you are looking at, is a direct, unified, manifestation of the divine essence that is all things.

Step 3 – Just sit.

Thoughts may still rise and fall, but ignore them. Let go of the sense that for you to experience the divine presence directly, you need to have fabulous visions, or see the future, or feel ecstasy. Remember, real love is unconditional. Love the divine as it is revealing itself to you right now in this moment. It may be an empty room, or the darkness of your closed eyes, or the steadiness of your breath, or the sunshine reflecting off the house next door. Do not shun the divine presence, just because it is appearing as it always has, seemingly mundanely, and openly. Look beyond appearances to the simplicity of the beingness in the moment.

This is why so many people fail to wake up or accept grace within their lives. They have a fairy tale of what it "should" look like. Love the divine for what it is, not for what you would like it to be. Wouldn't you ask the same of anyone else? Don't you want to be loved for what you are without any reservations, without having to put on a show, or having to act unnaturally? Why not show that same respect to the divine within and around you? Just as your heart would burst if you knew that kind of love, and you would smile from ear to ear, and your presence would radiate peace and warmth all around you, see how the divine presence responds in that same situation of unconditional love and acceptance.

We talk of Self-realization. What does that mean? It means we know the fullness of our being. We know we are beyond the mind, body, senses, time, space, etc. It means we know we exist, perpetually. We know we are eternally and immutably free, and that our only chains and bondage come from the concepts we adopt as true, and the defining characteristics we accept that we may experience a limited existence as a particular kind of being. But these are all just words with no corresponding meaning until you have direct experience of what this feels like. That is why we meditate and endeavor to practice a life that will harmonize our nervous systems and free our consciousness to have this direct experience. It is the spiritual practices that we choose that create the grooves that direct us back to the acceptance of our true nature.

We can say that meditation or spiritual practice doesn't work for us, but what we are really saying is that, it is not working on the time-scale we would like it to. Any authentic spiritual practice undertaken with the proper motive and surrender into the process will lift us up and out of our limited "character" that we have chosen to play in this lifetime. However, since we've chosen to play the game, we will of course come back to that character until the game is over. The free soul, has learned the rules, knows that he/she is identified with a particular chess piece on the board game of life, and is willing to be a good sport and play the game until the end. Once done, the free soul is awake, and can willingly choose if he/she would like to play again, or just exist in pure consciousness.

Self-realization directly experienced is what reveals to us the rules of the game we are playing and shows us the proper perspective from which we are playing it. We know we are not the chess piece; we are the hand that moves it. When the chess piece falls, we move on to another game, if we choose.

Spiritual Practice Experiencing Unity

When asked about the aim of spiritual practice, Ramana Maharshi said, "Removal of ignorance is the aim of practice, and not the acquisition of Realization. Realization is ever present, here and now. Were it to be acquired anew, Realization must be understood to be absent at one time, and present at another time. In that case, it is not permanent, and therefore not worth the attempt. But Realization is permanent and eternal and is here and now."

Again he was asked, "Grace is necessary for the removal of ignorance?"

Maharshi replied, "Certainly. But Grace is all along there. Grace is the Self. It is not something to be acquired. All that is necessary is to know its existence. For example, the sun is brightness only. He does not see darkness. Whereas others speak of darkness fleeing away on the sun approaching. Similarly, ignorance is also a phantom and not real. Because of its unreality, its unreal nature found, it is said to be removed.

"Again, the sun is there and also bright. You are surrounded by sunlight. Still, if you would know the sun you must turn your eyes in his direction and look at him. So also, Grace is found by practice alone although it is here and now."

If you want to know unity you must look at unity. You must not focus on separateness and variety. You see your next door neighbor, the tree outside, the computer in front of you, or your cat on the couch, and you say, "they are separate from me." You create separateness in this way. The first step to experiencing unity is to start accepting the notion that all that you experience is not separate, but is a continuous extension of your being.

In the autumn, when the leaves turn gold and orange and purple, you sit on a mountain top and a deep yearning arises to be one with nature and its beauty. This is separateness. Instead, see the colors, and the trees blowing in the wind, and smile. Accept that beauty as your very Self. You have dressed yourself in Autumn's splendor.

In meditation, you look on the face of your spiritual teacher or your depiction of the divine on the altar before you, and you long to know what that teacher knows or be one with that manifestation of God. You divide the wholeness. Instead, accept that what they know, you know, and you are expressing it through your particular life situation. Accept that you are as much a part of the divinity as your hand is to your elbow. They may be separated by a short physical distance, but they are a part of the same body. The hand and the elbow are equally important to have a working appendage. Do not judge what part of the body of God you may be. It is still the body of God.

In time, as your practice becomes stronger there is another practice to undertake. Now instead of working to change your ideas "that you are separate from all of life" to "accepting that you are one with all of life", you let go of even that. You no longer decide to say, "I am one with everything." You no longer label your oneness.

You simply experience life as it comes. No labeling, just experiencing. You surrender to the truth of your Self as all.

You no longer need words or concepts to prove it, or to remind yourself about it. You are IT! Another discourse with Ramana Maharshi will help to clarify this point. The quoted material is from Talks with Ramana Maharshi.

A devotee asked, "By the desire to surrender constantly, increasing grace is experienced, I hope?"

Maharshi replied, "Surrender once for all and be done with the desire [to surrender]. So long as the sense of doership is retained there is the desire; that is also personality. If this goes the Self is found to shine forth pure.

"The sense of doership is the bondage and not the actions themselves.

'Be still and know that I am God.' Here stillness is total surrender without a vestige of individuality. Stillness will prevail and there will be no agitation of mind. Agitation of mind is the cause of desire, the sense of doership and personality. If that is stopped there is quiet. There 'Knowing' means 'Being'. It is not the relative knowledge involving triads, knowledge, subject and object."

The devotee inquired at this, "Is the thought 'I am God' or 'I am the Supreme Being' helpful?"

Maharshi said, "'I am that I am.'

'I am' is God -- not thinking, 'I am God'.

Realize 'I am' and do not think I am.

'Know I am God' -- it is said, and not 'Think I am God.'"

So we see, from here, we must move from thinking to knowing. By meditation we clear the way to know directly. Knowing does not come from thinking or reasoning, it comes from having the capacity to experience what is, rather than our labels and ideas about what we'd like 'what is' to be.

In the next chapter we will explore specific advanced techniques useful to moving into this wisdom and Self-knowing. They may not be easy, but they are effective, and take practice, as with all things. Of course, your current meditation practice is helpful too, so long as you are intent and attentive to the procedure.

CHAPTER 11

PRACTICES FOR MOVING FULLY AS YOUR SELF

It has been said, if there was no self, there would be no problems. Why? Because everything that is a problem is in reference to something that a 'self', or a personality with a history, either wants or wants to avoid.

Let's consider the insects. Every day, I would conservatively believe, trillions of insects are eaten, run over, stepped on, poisoned, or killed in some way. They do not have a personality or a history as we humans do. They do not look around at all the 'senseless' death and say, "Why did this happen to my friends? What are we to learn from this slaughter!?"

No. They continue multiplying, eating, and doing what bugs do. It's not a problem for them.

Humans on the other hand feel very important. At this point in time, there are 7 billion of us, and that is a very small number compared to the staggering 10 quintillion (10,000,000,000,000,000,000) insects in the world, as estimated by Pulitzer Prize winner Dr. E. O. Wilson of Harvard University. It is this sense of importance that makes it all the harder to shake off our false sense of self.

To some, comparing humans to bugs seems absurd and callous. Why? Because some are very attached to their sense of self. That's fine. With that attachment comes potential suffering and confusion. If that's what they want, they can have it. They can continue the dream, that the unreal is real, and the real is absurd.

We have to remember, that when dreaming, the dream seems very real. If a loved one dies or leaves us in the dream, we cry painfully, and sometimes even wake up with terrible sadness ringing on. If we find a jewel worth millions of dollars, our elation is no less than if we were awake. We are dreaming even now.

There are people in this world who have either had a near-death experience, a spontaneous glimpse of awakening, or an awakening experience brought about through dedication to their spiritual practice. All of them testify to the reality that this life is but a dream. Once awake, all those things that seem so important fade away. Then a great peace descends, like a flood of light, and a knowing of immortality, eternity, and playfulness fills one's consciousness.

Higher Meaning, Order, Purpose and Significance - A Trap to Avoid

Once that peace descends, it is easy to say, yes, we are all just bugs spinning through an infinite cosmos, and smile, because the cosmos is beautiful, and it's not a problem to be an insignificant bug, because significance is not the point. If you want a point, it's the being, and the beauty of it all. And when folks who are still dreaming, point, and say, "You're crazy. Significance is the point! We have to find out the meaning of life! We need to find our purpose and BE somebody in this world! Etc. Etc. Etc." The awakened ones enjoy the display, knowing the dreamer is part of it all too.

If that is the case, you may ask, "Why ever search for a higher good or meaning or significance?" Is there a higher good if everything is consciousness? Not to my present knowledge. Saying there is a higher good, further creates categories and divisions in consciousness where there are none.

But...life is much easier for all involved when there is an order and a structure to things. Not being able to see the beauty of life all around and within, it is easy to fall into lethargy and say, "What's the point?" The inspiration towards a higher good, meaning and significance, is really an inspiration to realize the freedom of the Self, and the totality of Being. Many do not know that, and so philosophize or contemplate their higher purpose. This is good. Ultimately, they will realize their higher purpose is Being, harmony with the vastness of consciousness, and not a mental construct or moral dogma. Through philosophy, they will reach a point where realization dawns that mental concepts and constructs cannot provide the understanding they seek, and they will have to let go of the attachment to figuring things out through the mind. When they do, the light will shine through. Through contemplation, they are moving beyond the mind, into direct experience of Reality.

When in tune with the vastness of our consciousness (beyond the limited sense of self) we would naturally take care of our world and be supportive of others who have yet to realize what we realize, because it's all us anyway. Until we are in tune with the vastness and intelligence of our consciousness, we need to be told how to act, as if we were in tune with it. We are practicing.

Awakening is also not an excuse for anarchy. Having a functional, well-run government, allows the people of the world to relax, and trust that they are protected and cared for. Making healthy choices allows the body to run without making too much noise, comfortably, so the incarnated soul can explore consciousness and its wonders. To deny the trap of man-made significance, is not to deny that order and harmony are very good supports to awakening. When we have less disorder and chaos, it is easier to turn within, knowing that everything is well. This is why many awakened people promote scriptures and codes of conduct that keep us in line. A well-tended garden produces more enjoyable fruits, than one overrun by weeds and neglect.

Letting Go of Attachment to Emotions - We Are Not Our Emotions

Emotions are another matter to consider. Awakening is not to give the impression that once awake, you sit around like a fool on a hill, smiling benignly and ignoring reason and good sense. Although, once awake and free of attachment and aversion, you can do that if you want. My intention is to share that an awakened one sees the world, and can interact with it appropriately, but does not lose sight of the fact that it is a dream, a temporary play of light and shadow across the infinity of consciousness.

It is also good to realize that we do not have to become like a corpse, emotionless and cold. Emotions seem like an integral aspect of who we are, our sense of self. This is true to a degree. By reflecting on emotional habits and tendencies, we can say, yes, Sam, the personality, has a tendency to be happy when business is going well, and sad when it rains, and he gets angry when he hears about injustice in the world, and elated when he sees homeless people being fed.

Sam can be awake to his true nature, wearing the clothes of his personality and his emotional habits. The difference between an awakened Sam and one that is lost in identification with the dream, is that Awake Sam chooses to play the role we all know and love, being emotional in the ways we are used to. However, Awake Sam is not bound by that role. Meaning, he is not so identified with it, that he forgets that emotions and personality are just the play of consciousness. He can change and has the freedom to remove his emotional habits and tendencies at will, if it is not appropriate to what is happening right now. He also has the sensitivity and wisdom to know when playing his role, and stepping out of that role is appropriate.

If Sam wants, he can totally reinvent himself. He can decide he's had enough of his past habits and take actions to change them through relaxed will and consistent intention. He can reinvent himself, because he knows there is nothing all that important about the personality we call Sam. Although that personality may be enjoyable throughout its chosen duration.

This is a scary thought for many people. It is liberating for many others. The effect it has on you, is up to you.

Exercises To Have Your Own Direct Experience of this Knowledge

As mentioned above, this realization can occur from a near death experience, a spontaneous awakening episode, or through dedicated spiritual practice. Our emphasis is not to seek out near death experiences, or to wait around for a spontaneous awakening, but to do what works to ripen our consciousness through spiritual practice. If I wanted, I could sit around on a street corner waiting for some one to give me a million dollars, or I could get up and start earning money to work towards that goal. It's not impossible that someone, one day, might tune into my consciousness, and hand over the cash, as I sit on the cold hard concrete, but it's much more likely that I will reach that goal in this lifetime by taking appropriate action.

We've discussed many topics in this course that will help to harmonize the life and better prepare the ground of our consciousness for awakening. Review past chapters to strengthen your understanding of these processes. The following exercises, performed daily, will further purify your consciousness on deeper levels.

You must stick with them and not give up. As many enlightened teachers have said, "It is better to dig one deep well, when in search of water, than to dig hundreds of shallow ones." If the mind gets bored or says, "You just haven't found the right technique, keep looking." Ignore it. You are not the mind. Keep going until you have realized what you are.

Always remember, meditation techniques serve to engage your attention, to build up the strength of your concentration, so you can hold your awareness on a point until realization dawns. When our attention is weak and every distraction disrupts our focus, we must practice a technique. As time goes by, our attention grows stronger. No longer do we care how bright the room is, or how loud the people outside are, or how many thoughts we have, or how we have a little emotional unrest inside. We can remove our awareness from these things, and sink it into the Self. With each movement of our awareness in the Self, we gain direct knowledge of the fullness of our being. When all that knowledge has been integrated, we are awake.

These advanced techniques are more easily practiced after you have proficiency in mantra or breathe awareness, and you can easily calm your mind and emotions. Don't despair if you are still working on developing your attention, or calming your mind and emotions. Everyone has to learn how to do it. It's part of the process.

Spiritual practice is very good, but it is not a substitute for working out mental, psychological or emotional disturbances. It is best to work those out with a professional, and save your spiritual work for just that, spiritual growth. If you have mental, psychological, or emotional difficulties, regular spiritual practice may help you move through them, but that is not the point of spiritual practice. This kind of work is for a person who has taken care of themselves in the outer world, so they can turn within without mental, psychological or emotional distraction.

Mundane example: Meditation is not going to fix my plumbing, but I guarantee a plumber will. Sitting around meditating on having functional plumbing is a waste of time when a simple phone call will work. Then once the plumber has done his job, I don't have to worry about the plumbing anymore and can direct my attention to the Self. Nor will meditation fix my bad relationship. Finding a supportive partner, or finding a counselor to help with my lack of self-worth will. Then I can meditate easier, because I'm not thinking about my bad relationships. Make sense?

Once you are accustomed to being settled and turning within, begin adding one of these practices to your sitting meditation on a regular basis.

Advanced Meditation Practices

Breathing Through the Spine

Step 1 -- After sitting quietly for a while in meditation, turn your attention to your spine and the space between the eyebrows. Imagine there is a hollow tube running through the spine, from the base of the spine, up through the spine, up through the skull and ending at the spiritual eye, the space between the eyebrows.

Step 2 -- Begin breathing slightly deeper, in a comfortable and relaxed manner. Maintaining your attention on the spine and spiritual eye.

Step 3 -- Now, link the breath to the spine. As you inhale, imagine you are pulling a current of energy up through the spine. It can feel like cool water ascending up the spine to the spiritual eye.

Step 4 -- On the exhale, imagine that same current of energy flowing down from the spiritual eye like water—warm, soothing, and relaxing. Remain attentive, upright and alert, but let your being relax with each repetition. Let go of the external world, and move deeper into the Self.

Step 5 — After a comfortable duration (don't strain) of this practice, take another deep inhale, and pull the energy up to the spiritual eye. Then keep your attention at the spiritual eye, feeling that energy there, and let your breath return to normal. Now you are just sitting quietly with your relaxed attention at the space between the eyebrows.

Step 6 — Stay relaxed and attentive in this way until the end of your meditation. Then go about your day.

Listening to Silence

Listening to the silence is a very good practice. If we could just do this, that would be all we would ever need to do. Why don't more teachers advise it? It can be difficult. It is often hard enough for people to hold their attention on a mantra or visualization, imagine the difficulty focusing on the absence of sound. The good news is that listening to silence is not exactly what the words imply. We are actually listening *to* something.

Step 1 — After a duration of quiet, relaxing and alert meditation, bring your awareness up to your crown. Simply feel the area at the top of your head, and/or just above your head.

Step 2 — Keeping your feeling at the crown, become aware of your sense of hearing. Listen to the silence in the room, or just around your head. Do you hear a faint sound, such as a high-pitched constant tone, or an electrical frequency? Give your attention to that sound.

Step 3 — Hold your attention on this sound for a minute or two. If you are like most people, your attention will easily wander. Stay focused and gently bring your attention back to the sound as many times as you have to.

Step 4 — Now listen deeper. Do you hear a different tone or frequency behind or within the sound you initially heard? If so, direct your attention to that sound. If not, stay with the initial sound. Listen for another minute or two.

Step 5 — Listen deeper again. Has the sound shifted, changed or deepened? Give your awareness to this sound. Stay listening to this for a minute or two.

Step 6 -- Continue this process of listening deeper to the sound behind the sound you are hearing. Keep gently returning your attention back to the process, no matter how many times you get distracted. Keep your attention at the crown, throughout the process.

When you begin this practice, be easy on your self. Do it when you are well settled, and in a fairly quiet environment. As your attention grows stronger, and you can go deeper and deeper into this sound, you may eventually become aware of a sound, like the roaring of an ocean, all the while aware of nothing else but being this sound.

You are listening to the OM vibration. By listening deeply, you are following this vibration back to its source, which is pure consciousness, your true nature.

Do not overly engage your mind or analyze techniques. They are for the process of strengthening your concentration and ripening your consciousness. Practice your daily meditations without attachment to the results. Simply do it. Don't think about it.

Then after meditation, read a scripture that is sacred to you or speaks to you. If you like analysis, analyze what you are reading. Try to understand the clear intention of the author.

In this way, you ripen your consciousness through meditation, and then when you have a direct experience of Self-revealed knowledge, you will have the information from reading the scripture to help you make sense of it.

The words you read about spiritual growth are only to serve as sign posts. That way, when you have a certain experience, the information you gathered from study, allows you to make sense of your process. Always remember, ***the real power comes from daily spiritual practice***.

CHAPTER 12

WHAT TO DO WHEN YOU ARE NOT TRANQUIL

We will begin this chapter with a discussion between Nisargadatta Maharaj, a 20th century master, and a student. The following is from the book, "*I AM THAT*".

Questioner: I have met many realized people, but never a liberated man. Have you come across a liberated man, or does liberation mean, among other things, also abandoning the body?

Maharaj: What do you mean by realization and liberation?

Q: By realization I mean a wonderful experience of peace, goodness and beauty, when the world makes sense and there is an all-pervading unity of both substance and essence. While such experience does not last, it cannot be forgotten. It shines in the mind, both as memory and longing. I know what I am talking about, for I have had such experiences. By liberation I mean to be permanently in that wonderful state. What I am asking is whether liberation is compatible with the survival of the body.

M: What is wrong with the body?

Q: The body is so weak and short-lived. It creates needs and cravings. It limits one grievously.

M: So what? Let the physical expressions be limited. But liberation is of the Self from its false and self-imposed ideas; it is not contained in some particular experience, however glorious.

As touched on earlier in this text, there is often the idea that tranquility and liberation of consciousness indicate a glorified human condition. Sometimes, even when established in the Self, violent waves or turbulence may arise on the surface of consciousness, either in the form of health challenges, relationship confusion, financial disparity, societal discord, or any other number of unpleasant circumstances. The questioner, in the above passage, indicates that he thinks liberation means abiding permanently in a wonderful state. The Maharaj reminds him that liberation is abidance in the Self, and not abiding in identification with the changing phenomena the Self may witness.

Interacting in a world, through a mind and body, we have limitations. As it says in the Yoga Sutras in chapter 3 on Soul Powers, the reason we do not know everyone else's thoughts, is because that would result in confusion of minds. Here limitation is necessary. It does not say, we cannot know other people's thoughts, only that we don't, to avoid confusion.

We do not exist in this world as completely unlimited, because we have agreed to play a role. If there was no limitation to our roles, confusion would result, and nothing would ever get done, nor would any karma get exhausted.

Liberation being of the Self, we can turn within, know and be our real nature, yet return to the world to play our part as it is necessary. Often we do not want to play our parts, because it is not glorious, or wonderful, or like all the wonderful dramas on TV. The interesting thing to remember, is that all those dramas on TV are imagination, and not real. We try to shape reality to match a fantasy, which is distinctly different. Our real nature is beyond all of this. It is not fooled by fantasy, nor is it bound by 'reality'. It simply is. And in that "is-ness" resides beauty, love, and wisdom.

Our stories, our history, our past, those thoughts we habitually think, are those limitations with which we identify. They are also the reasons we do not allow ourselves to be happy. As Eckhart Tolle has said, "Listen to people's stories and they could all be entitled 'Why I Cannot Be at Peace Now.'"

We can say things like:

"I cannot be at peace now, because I am not with that special someone."

"I cannot be at peace now, because I don't have enough information to be enlightened."

"I cannot be at peace now, because I am confused about some areas of my life."

"I cannot be at peace now, because I am dying."

"I cannot be at peace now, because I am alive, and want to be dead."

"I cannot be at peace now, because I don't have a cigarette."

"I cannot be at peace now, because I have no money."

"I cannot be at peace now, because I have all the money in the world, and am still missing something."

"I cannot be at peace now, because I had an unhappy childhood."

The stories that are possible in this world are vast and endless. This is precisely why our stories don't matter when it comes to tranquility. It is also why, even if we are not tranquil, we learn to let go of identification with tranquility, in order to remain there. Attachment to peace and tranquility is still attachment. Imagine if everything in your life was perfect, and yet for a moment or an hour or two you become angry, depressed, agitated. Or maybe for a day, or a month or a year, you were sick. Rather than letting it pass, which it will do one way or another, you dwell. Then, once it passes you continue dwelling, trying to figure out what it was all about. Why did you have that passing mood? Why did you get sick?

Tranquility is shaken, and we continue shaking it, even after the un-tranquil situation passes. This is not to say, that if you have a problem, you shouldn't figure out what is causing it so you can avoid future experiences of that problem. However, you can usually tell if a problem is worth using energy to explore if it recurs. For example, if you have one bad relationship, but the rest were good, chances are, it isn't much to worry about. If you have one bad relationship after another, that might be an indication to explore possible causes and remedies. If you fall and bruise your leg, and yet for the past twenty years, you have almost a perfect record of not falling, you can let that one pass too. However, if you find that throughout your life, you've been clumsy, that might be an indication that you could explore and remedy that problem.

What's the answer to "What do I do when I'm not tranquil, or when things don't work out exactly as my expectations would suggest?" Let it pass.

Kriya Yoga teacher Roy Eugene Davis, once told a story of a person who wrote to him. The writer had mentioned how Mr. Davis writes and speaks about realizing our immortality and eternal life. The writer then went on to say, how he found it a depressing possibility that he could potentially live forever. The problem there, was that the writer was identified with his life situation. Mr. Davis, was not speaking about the immortality of the life situation.

This is a common problem that many spiritual aspirants face. They do not understand what it means to be spiritually liberated or to exist in tranquility, because they do not have a very good memory of what that is like. They don't remember what it is like to be identified with the immortal sense of "I Am". All they remember is the immediate, limited, life situation.

When we first learn to meditate, we are learning to calm the mind and emotions and to refine the nervous system to be able to process clearer states of consciousness. When we first adopt recommended lifestyle routines at the beginning of our spiritual path, we are making choices to cut back on the amount of distractions we will have in life, so we can direct our energy to remembering and re-establishing our consciousness in the timeless "I Am".

After this becomes stable, we then dive deep, practicing holding our awareness as the "I Am". It is this practice, and they call it practice for a reason, that allows us to exist freely, because we then know what we are, beyond any doubt. We can also exist as we are, without doubt. When this realization dawns, we know. No matter what anyone else says, or what the doubts of anyone else may be, we are unmoved by them. Just as no one could make you doubt that a ripe red apple is sweet, no one could shake you from the realization of your Self.

How is this done?

First we make sure our meditation practice is stable. This means we meditate every day with alert, yet relaxed intention. We have found a technique or an understanding of what it takes to calm down the mind and emotions. That may include determining activities, foods, or personal interactions that get your mind and emotions spinning, and minimizing their influence.

If you want to be Self-realized and Tranquil, you need to realize that meditation is an excellent tool for that, but it must be understood properly. There is a stage beyond experiencing peacefulness that needs to be activated for optimal benefits.

In stage two, you begin doing your best to exist as the "I Am". This is the state beyond:

"I am meditating."

"I am a personality."

"I have these likes and dislikes."

"My breathe is quiet."

"I am in a still room."

You move to the simple experience of the room where you are sitting. You simply experience the thoughts that rise and fall in your mind.

You simply feel a passing emotion or memory. All the while, you are aware. You are not aware as being identified with anything in particular. You are aware of your Self as the witnessing presence. You can't see it. You can't feel it. You can only be it.

You can drive your awareness deeper. With eyes closed, in a very quiet room, you imagine withdrawing your awareness from your senses. As you do this, memories, thoughts and emotions now become "external." You drive your awareness deeper, withdrawing your awareness from even these subjective internalized (yet still external from the vantage point of the Self) perceptions.

This takes dedication and practice. Sometimes it feels like it takes lots of energy and concentration. The rewards are worth it. Even if you pull your awareness only to the level of being aware of the memories, emotions and memories, that is good. Keep endeavoring to pull it deeper. One day, you will withdraw even from that! If only for a second or two, it is progress. You continue, until it becomes natural and easy.

As you get used to holding your awareness on this sense of "I Am". It becomes easy. You have been practicing so long, that you can hold your awareness there effortlessly, because you know how it's done. Just like driving a car may seem like a big task if you've never driven one, with practice you hardly have to think about it. Be patient yet consistent. Continue practicing, and letting your self grow stronger in concentration at your own rate. We all take to this work with varying backgrounds and abilities, but we all reach the same state.

When All Else Fails

Sometimes we try. We use our self-effort. We apply all the knowledge that we have, and yet we still fall into a space of sorrow or unconsciousness. When this occurs, a very good practice is learning to surrender into grace. Now grace is our very own nature, and so we are essentially surrendering into our Self. But we only fall into sorrow when we cannot shake free of the feeling of being limited as an individualized being, a personality, a history, a series of expectations that needs fulfilled. We are much vaster than all of that. Surrendering into grace is surrendering into that vastness that is omnipotent and omniscience and forever established in love and wisdom. At least, that is the closest words can come to what it feels like.

How is it done? Wherever you are, you let go. You may be in pain, or in an uncomfortable situation that you desperately wish to be different. You may be in a life situation and suddenly find yourself wanting to be in a much better place, or maybe you suddenly discover another avenue in life that is more in line with your expression as a divine being of love, yet you have a history, and obligations, and commitments that need fulfilling. You cannot see your self changing overnight, yet you desperately feel the calling. You let go, and surrender into the vastness of your being. The little you can do nothing. You know, because you've tried, or you've found your self too paralyzed to move.

Remember a time when you got a rock or a bug in your eye. It burns and hurts. Your friend says, "Hey, I'll help you out." Yet every time they make a move to take the offending object out of your eye, you flinch, close your eyes and pull away. Sure it may hurt a little more as the object is removed, but if you relax, then in an instant, you can see again, and the sting is gone. That same mechanism that would allow you to surrender to that aid, is the same mechanism, or feeling state that accompanies surrender.

Whether it be in meditation, or prayer, or in daily living, when you have done your best, and you cannot conceive of anything more you could do, try letting go. Surrender, knowing the rest of you, the universe, will move in such a way to either make the crooked roads straight, or provide the wisdom to understand your situation with clarity. This may take practice, but it is well worth the effort. Give it a try when you are not tranquil, and don't fight it when your tranquility comes rushing back to you quicker than your little self thinks it deserves.

Thought for the day: "Not even the very wise can see all ends."

CHAPTER 13

AWARENESS THROUGHOUT THE DAY

The weather bothers many people. You may have noticed, that sometimes it is too cold, or too hot, or too humid or too dry. No matter what state the weather is in, someone can complain about it. The weather patterns are caused by a multitude of factors, such as time of year, solar activity, the movement of tectonic plates, the flapping of a sparrow's wings, your car ride to work.

Our life experiences are like those weather patterns. Sometimes it rains when we want to play outside. Sometimes the sun shines beautifully when we are stuck at a desk finishing a report.

Sometimes it's fifty degrees and all the snow has melted on the weekend of our ski trip. Sometimes our weddings take place during the perfect breeze and bluest skies. Sometimes our fishing trips couldn't be more crisp and temperate.

Our minds are like those weather patterns. Some days we are struck with motivation and courage. Other days, we are despondent and don't see the point. Some days we are in love, and not a thing can go wrong. Other days, our anger comes out at the drop of a hat.

Just like the weather patterns, our life experiences and mental states are often the result of an infinite number of factors. Our past choices influence our future experiences. Our collection of negative experiences, turns our mind darker. An abundance of luck and opportunity, keeps us thinking positively. The planets, past lives, any thing we can imagine, can have an effect on our experiences and our mind.

These are all external factors. A child sees thunder, lightning and rain outside and protests, "But I don't want to go outside! I don't want to get wet!". An adult sees the same weather patterns, and reaches for her rain coat, umbrella and rain boots. She goes about her day, and still doesn't get wet. A child sees ice and snow across the land, and says, "But I don't want to get cold! Don't make me go out there." The adult puts on his winter jacket, wool hat, gloves and insulated boots. He goes about his day, warm. Note, the weather didn't matter. What mattered was the response.

As we grow in wisdom, we learn that we do not necessarily need to be overly influenced by the weather patterns of life situations or mental states, just as we do not need to be unduly influenced by the weather patterns of nature. Now, it is obvious that some "severe weather" needs to be respected, no matter what the case, but all-in-all, with wisdom we learn how to move through life and take the necessary and useful actions to prevent the weather from slowing down our lives.

Meditation

On numerous occasions, I have experienced the power of meditation to change my state of consciousness. I may have been experiencing a passing sadness, frustration, or confusion. Not knowing what else to do, I meditated. I used the techniques I know, with intention, and really gave my self to the process.

After completing the techniques I sat in the silence, with my attention in the higher brain centers (The Spiritual Eye and Crown of the Head). Almost like magic, I felt the mood lift. I felt my confusion replaced with an inspiration to take action in some way. The very act of sitting, meditating and waiting, cleared away what ever temporary storm cloud was blinding me at present.

Waiting in the silence is where the transformation occurs. You practice the technique to reign in your scattered awareness. Your awareness has lost its power because it is focused on too many "what if's" or "could be's". From here, the moods can settle in, because the awareness is not concentrated or light enough to move through or rise above them.

Once the awareness is concentrated by the practice, it has risen above the influence of the difficulties you perceive. From this "higher" vantage point, your much vaster Self, with connections to the wholeness and wisdom of life can send a breeze of inspiration, to get your ship back on course. Your inner tranquility resumes its rightful place as the center of your awareness.

Short Term Spiritual Memory & Long Term Spiritual Memory

Have you ever been in a physical situation you did not like? Have you ever been ill or injured? Have you ever found yourself in a relationship that was draining and debilitating? Have you ever been in an unsafe environment? What did you do in these situations? Hopefully, you acknowledged your present circumstance, and then looked for a way out or a solution to your circumstance.

I've noticed that in situations like this, when there is difficulty in the external world, most healthy-minded people seem to remember that before the difficulty arose, there was a peacefulness and happiness in their life. They do what is necessary to return their experience to that natural state of ease. If they are sick, they go to the doctor. If they are in an unsafe environment, they leave. If relationships are harmful, they cut the relationship off and find more pleasant people. There is a sense of memory here. By remembering that there was a time when things were comfortable and good, we do what is necessary to restore that equilibrium.

I have also noticed, that, even in seemingly healthy-minded people, there can be a disconnect in this process, when it comes to their mental/emotional/spiritual states. Let us say that a mood comes upon a person. Suddenly, the person cannot even imagine what it was like to be happy and calm. Their minds sink into quick sand and they are paralyzed. They forget that just an hour before they were happily moving through life. Now they are in darkness, and they do nothing to move through it. They sit in the darkness.

From a spiritual perspective, there are times when our minds are filled with light and wisdom and our intuition is humming as we move spontaneously in the world. Then for whatever reason, our wisdom shuts down. Once again, we are stuck in mental patterns that prevent us from accepting the wholeness of life as our very being. We start making decisions from a fearful, unbalanced point of view.

It is common to think that we have no control over these situations and that we just have to ride them out. This thought creates that reality. Then we are helpless and adrift on a sea of uncertainties with no tools or instruments to guide and steer our course. The reality is that as we are embodied, we will be subject to cosmic weather patterns. The reality also is that there have been countless awakened souls in this world, who have realized this. They created, for us, umbrellas, rain coats, winter jackets, scarves, gloves, boots, etc, for us to move through those weather patterns. These are in the forms of meditation techniques and awareness practices, scriptures and wisdom.

A deeper factor of confusion, is identification with our STATES of consciousness, rather than identification with consciousness itself. When you are in a bad relationship, or in an unsafe environment, it is easier, to know, "Hey, this isn't who I am. In fact, this is dangerous to my embodied self, so I am going to get out of here!" Since our thoughts, emotions and states of consciousness, seem to be internal, as if they are who we are, it is not so easy to shake those off. Why would you want to shake our 'self' off anyway?

Our emotional states, common thought patterns, and regular states of consciousness are the building blocks of what we call the personality. The personality is really just the organized pattern of behavioral characteristics that your 'soul' is expressing through. Yet, from the time we were children, we are taught this is who we are, and that we have to defend and sustain this 'character'. After that we go through life trying to sustain this idea of our self. We come upon a situation where we need to act out of character, because it is appropriate, and we do not. We maintain our idea, at the expense of being inappropriate.

Imagine that you have been taught that you are a good person. You are nice and kind to everybody. You make everyone feel good and give them what they want. It is totally out of character for you to do anything to hurt someone else's feelings. You have been accepting and reaffirming this personality for 45 years. Yet, one day you meet a person who is cruel to you and is about to cause you a lot of problems. Your personality is strong! You feel dissonance, "but I should be nice to everyone", you think. I should give this person what he wants, because to deny it, would make him feel bad. It's five years later and you are now in a codependent relationship with someone who always professes they love you, yet by their actions often makes you feel bad, either through verbal or physical abuse. You don't leave, because that would make them feel bad. They love you after all, and you are not a personality that makes waves.

That is a bit of an extreme example, but it happens on some level every day to nearly every one. Because we are more interested in sustaining a consistent personality, we create more and more problems for our selves and the world.

This occurs, because we have forgotten that we are not our thoughts, emotions, reactions, and states of consciousness. We have forgotten that we are the consciousness, the space, in which all of these things manifest and then fade away.

By listening to an awakened person, or noting how they move through life, we can see that no matter the circumstance, it is possible to remain balanced, poised, calm and even peaceful. This is our natural state. We can pay close attention (closer than even our infatuation with discord) to those times in our lives when everything feels right and in harmony. We can note how we feel after being with an even-minded person, or in a holy environment, or on top of a mountain with the quiet sun shining on us, or how we feel after a deep meditation. We can remember, this is our natural state. We can reclaim it as our natural state.

When the cosmic weather patterns change, and we notice a frustration, anxiety, discord, anger, or despondency creeping across our awareness, we can acknowledge it. We do not claim it for ourselves, or even define ourselves by it. We can say, "Ahh, here comes some rain and hail in the form of this state." We simply acknowledge the weather pattern rolling in.

Then we can ask, "Since I am familiar with this state, what might be a good thing for me to do so I can go about my life naturally, without being unduly influenced by it?" You pause to contemplate for a moment. You remember that the last time you felt a depression coming on, that it helped to go to the gym and work out. You noticed you felt one hundred times better after that. You may remember that the last time you were feeling overwhelmed and confused you went into your meditation chamber, and meditated, prayed, and asked for divine grace to flow through and assist. You remember that afterwards, you were able to deal with your situation more easily.

The main point of all of this is to start giving more attention to the times when you feel calm, collected and aware, and remember those times. When your internal environment starts to develop some unpleasant weather patterns, you begin to acknowledge that those internal difficulties do not define you. From there you remember what helped you deal with those situations in the past, and then take action. Develop your-long term spiritual memory.

Every Moment

Every moment there is awareness. Every moment, you are aware of something. That doesn't mean that you remember everything from every moment, but know you are always there.

Within this manifesting world, change is the constant. Some experiences seem very repetitious and similar from day to day, but the fact is that no moments are exactly the same. Not even your personality, no matter how hard you hold on to it, is the same from day to day.

We can take this knowledge and accept it. Now our expectations will not be shattered. We know the truth. We know that trying to recreate anything from the past is futile. We stop wasting our time in that way. We stop imagining that if only we had the right combination of ingredients we could return to that state that was so wonderful before.

Now that our awareness is free of expectations and the wrong use of our imagination, it becomes empowered. It's energy can be directed to what is actually happening around us. We can see with clear vision. We can respond to the changing world with confidence and precision.

Picture someone on the ocean waiting to surf. They are out on the ocean waiting for a wave. Yet their mind is absorbed in that one perfect wave they rode three years ago. All of their thought is bent on feeling that slight warm breeze from the south that preceded that perfect wave. They are watching the horizon, waiting for the sun to hit the magic degree that brought about the beautiful experience. And as they wait for the re-creation of this long past, now unreal experience, wave after lovely rolling wave passes them by. The surfer misses the thrill of thousands of waves that are actually there, all because of absorption in the past, a now unreal reality.

When we are identified with simple awareness of our consciousness we respond appropriately to every circumstance, and see clearly the current state of reality around us. Whatever you experience throughout the day, let it flow through you. Do not latch on to it, or try to identify with it. If you are going to identify with anything, let it be the space in which all your experiences occur. This also applies to your internal experiences.

Your thoughts, emotions, memories, and states of consciousness arise within you, yet you are the space in which they arise.

At first this can feel wrong or unnatural. That is only because you are used to identifying with circumstances and personality traits. I'm not saying it's easy either. It takes practice. If it helps, remember those times when you were in deep sleep. There was no personality or thought there, yet YOU persisted. So you can survive this. You will not cease to exist.

That is often the common fear. Your personality may change its state, into something more wholesome, and in tune with the infinite, and by that standard, the "you" you know will cease to exist. But the real you always remains.

(Note: You can say that you did not exist in deep sleep, but it's not true. If you didn't exist then, how you are still existing now? It's more appropriate to say that you don't remember existing in deep sleep. If you think back about three days ago, do you remember every second and every action that you took? Just because you don't remember existing then, doesn't mean you didn't.)

Practicing a Single Truth

A useful tool we can use throughout our lives to move us into this state of awareness and tranquility is practicing a single truth.

According to Vasistha's Yoga we can experience tranquility and an enlightened state by adopting one of two mental positions. The first mental position is, "I am nothing. Nothing I see, experience or do, is me." The second mental position is, "I am everything. Every thought, action, person, God, Goddess, experience, creature and thing is me."

#1 "I Am Nothing"

According to Nisargadatta Maharaj, to hold to the mental position that "I am nothing", is wisdom. You become the space in which all things occur, and then not even that. You are awareness itself. You are aware of everything that passes through your field, yet you know it is not you. No longer identifying with anything, when things change, you are not disturbed. You are free.

#2 "I Am Everything"

According to Nisargadatta Maharaj, to hold the mental position that "I am everything", is love. Now there is nothing which you are not. No matter what anyone does to you, you are doing it to yourself. No matter the weather patterns, it's ok. It's just you anyway. Every concept of the divine is your very self. The smallest atom, to the vastness of the universe is you. You are doing everything, because you are everything. Here your mind can expand beyond its small confines, and thought itself becomes unnecessary, because as you can see, everything is happening without thought anyway!

What does this do to the mind?

Our problems arise when the mind becomes engaged. We believe, we have to think about things, figure things out. We try, and sometimes our conclusions line up with experience, and sometimes they fall far from the mark, and often we notice that correlation between the two is random.

The mind is for storing information. It is for balancing your check book, writing a coherent letter, planning a house, or calculating a physics equation. The mind is not meant for figuring things out beyond remembering and calculating.

If you hold the state that "I am nothing", then you have nothing to think about. Your thinking doesn't matter. You are in neutral, being nothing. You find that the world continues, even without your thoughts to validate it. Thoughts still arise. You still get up in the morning and make bacon and eggs for breakfast. Yet, none of this is you. You don't have to think about it anymore. It happens.

If you hold the state that "I am everything", then you don't have to think about interacting with the world in particular ways. It's all you. You continue to learn and grow and change, and yet your thoughts don't matter, because it happens anyway. You still exist as everything. If someone gives you a million dollars, you don't have to think about why you deserved it. You gave it to yourself. If someone runs into your car, you don't have to contemplate what karma led to this, it was just something you felt like doing at that time.

Now the mind will resist and rail against this. You may even think this is total nonsense and a good way to get out of responsibility for your actions. Well, according to the Gita, you are not the doer of anything anyway. God is the doer. When you claim responsibility, you claim karma. Then you have to suffer the good and bad of your fate. If you are everything or nothing, then it doesn't matter, you experience yourself, as it is. No need for judgment, or reasons.

This does not indicate that you will become a base and vile person either. *The natural impulse of consciousness is towards harmony and peace. When you give up identification with mind, through consistent practice of one of these truths, you will find that your actions are actually in accord with a higher process.*

Think of nature. The flowers grow. The cows eat the grass. The lions eat the cows. The sun shines. The clouds rain. Sometimes those flowers are weeds, and sometimes they are roses. Sometimes the cows are clearing a field, and sometimes they are destroying it. Sometimes the lion is providing food for his young, and sometimes he is removing a sick or lame animal from the herd. Sometimes the sun shines and brings life to the marigolds, and sometimes the sun scorches the earth and kills people with heat stroke. Sometimes the rains water the gardens, and sometimes they swell the rivers and destroy villages. That is what happens.

If you want to burden your self with responsibility and karma, you are welcome to it. It is your mind that tricks you into thinking this little person is so important, that your responsibility will truly make a difference. By practicing a single truth, until you know it fully as reality, the mind cannot keep a hold on you. Then you move beyond the mind and act with the same grace and naturalness as the natural world. You realize the "little you" is an expression of the wholeness of life and its cycles. From this knowledge, your awareness expands until it is fully absorbed by the you that is the wholeness of life itself.

This may seem overwhelming, or far beyond your current scope of understanding. That's fine. You have to start somewhere and this is the starting point. Contemplate which one of those truths you feel you resonate with most easily. Then write it down in a place you will see it often. Put it in your meditation space too. Put it beside your bed. Put it anywhere you spend a lot of time.

Then, moment by moment, day by day, year by year, imagine your truth as a reality for you. Explore what you might feel like if it were true, right now. Dedicate yourself to its practice. You will find as you ripen, the implication of the truth will dawn within your understanding. You will know its reality, just as assuredly as you know yourself as a man or a woman. It won't be a thought or a concept, but a direct experience.

In this way, every moment of your day becomes imbued with tranquility, and divine remembrance.

CHAPTER 14

BEYOND THE COSMIC WEATHER PATTERNS

When you've seen beyond your self, you will find peace of mind waiting there.
-George Harrison

I imagine a homeless person spends a great deal of time looking for shelter. A person with the means to procure shelter does not. Someone with shelter has additional freedom to explore other aspects of life, such as finding food, or sleeping soundly out of the elements. Meditation and internalization of attention serves to build a spiritual shelter from our mental/emotional and cosmic weather patterns.

Once built we are then free to explore meaningful matters, such as our relationship to the divine, our life purpose, and the totality of our being. We move from simply looking for an escape from our mental-emotional torment or spiritual vapidness, to diving head first into the richness of exploring a divine, and very much alive consciousness, which is our own Self.

When we do not have a meditation practice it is easy for us to be shaken by our mental/emotional weather patterns. If you have a consistent meditation practice, and you still get easily disturbed mentally and emotionally, try not meditating for a few days. You will then appreciate the benefits of your practice more thoroughly. You may realize through this fast from meditation, that while your current shelter (meditation practice) may have a leaky roof, or very noticeable draft, that it is much preferred to no shelter at all! Take this as an opportunity to patch up the points in your practice that may need repair. Then you can look forward to a very satisfying spiritual exploration.

Assessing Your Current Practice

If you are like most spiritual aspirants in search of tranquility, spiritual peace and inner wisdom, you have been meditating for a while. You have noticed that your life has improved a bit. You're not so touchy, or irritable. You smile more. You understand much more of the spiritual literature that you read. Yet, you may still feel as though you haven't broken through to that direct connection that the spiritual master's experience. You may still feel separate from the totality of being (God). You may feel like your inner guidance and knowing isn't what it really could be. Arriving at this point in your evolution, it is advised to take a close look at your practice, to properly and honestly assess your efforts.

Check List for Assessing Your Spiritual Shelter

#1 Is Your Practice Simple?

Ask your self, "Do I have two or three techniques that I can use consistently to calm my mind and emotions? Or do I jump around from one technique to another, thinking there is something wrong with the technique, since I'm not getting the results I want?"

Since the year 2000, I have used about three techniques consistently. They are simple. They are not complicated. They get results.

When I practice a technique, I give my full attention to it. When I repeat a mantra, I endeavor to sink all of my attention on listening to that sound within my awareness. If other thoughts arise, I brush it aside, and return to the mantra. I do this over and over and over again, no matter how many distractions arise. Then in a few minutes or even sometimes an hour, super-consciousness dawns. I am thought free and existing in the silence.

What made this work? Was it the special meaning of the words? Was it that I got lucky? No. It was that I decided that I was going to glue my attention on this one word phrase (the mantra), letting all distractions pass until my inner peace was unveiled.

By "ignoring distractions" or "letting them pass", I like to use the idea of walking through a forest. You want to get from where you are, a normal mental state, to where you want to be, a clear mental state. We can look at this as though we are moving from point A to point B within a forest. In between point A and point B, there are rocks, trees, fallen logs, vines, poison ivy, streams, and shrubs. These are like your meditation distractions.

When you want to get from point A to point B in a forest, you start walking (using your meditation technique). When you come upon a fallen log, you step over it. When you come upon a stream, you jump over it. etc. You don't make it into a big deal.

You pass them by, giving them very little thought, and you most definitely stop thinking about them, once you have moved beyond them. Treat the mental, emotional and physical distractions you experience during meditation like this. Keep your eye on the technique, while moving through the distractions without too much engagement of your attention.

#2 Are There Stressful Situations in Your Life that You Can Change?

It's hard to meditate when you are under the pressure of a difficult relationship, have extreme money complications or have poor health. There is a reason that, in the past, a person accepted in a spiritual tradition had to be a monk, nun, or renunciate type. By giving up all the things in life that cause most of our drama (relationships, money, sex, work, addictions, etc.), spiritual aspirants of the past, had seemingly less hurdles to overcome. Luckily, in this day and age, anyone with a little sense can have a comfortable home, a healthy body, and a decent work situation that doesn't take up too much of their vital energy to maintain.

Ask your self, "Am I serious about wanting to experience spiritual growth and tranquility in my life?" If your answer is "Yes, of course I am." Then when you have people in your life that cause you grief, stress, and heartache on a consistent basis, and this gets in the way of having a satisfying meditation practice, you will have no problem moving on from that relationship, or at least adjusting to it, to avoid this unneeded distraction. You have your priorities straight, right?

Remember, you can't experience what the masters experience if you are caught up in emotional turmoil every time you sit down to meditate. Our goal, in regards to this course, is to assist your awakening process to fully unqualified happiness, peace and knowledge that the masters know. It is not to provide a crutch that allows you to continue in relationship that depletes your soul force. You can meditate and reset your system as often as you like after every bad relationship encounter. But that isn't propelling you onward to higher realizations.

This same idea applies to proper dietary and exercise choices (or lack thereof). It applies to work that constantly puts you under unpleasant strain, and wears you down. It basically applies to anything that takes up your time, that you can avoid through cognitive or behavioral change.

#3 Do You Get Enough Rest?

Is it common that when you meditate, your head bobs, you find your self caught in daydreams, you fall asleep easily as soon as your body starts to relax from the process, or your awareness seems very dull and you cannot concentrate? This may be an indication that you need more sleep or to under take some stress management measures to get your energy back.

Consider taking a nap? Yes, it's fine to take a nap, and it doesn't have to mean something is wrong with you. Consider going to sleep earlier. You may have to rearrange your day or cut out some activities to make this possible. Remember, your desire is for spiritual freedom, so you are willing to make this sacrifice. Proper rest may very well be the first step, that turns your meditation from a dull, half awake revelry, to an enlightening and enlivening process that jump starts your life and spiritual growth.

#4 How Do You Feed Your Mind and Senses?

When you are not meditating, what do you do with your time? What kinds of books do you read? What kind of places do you frequent? What TV shows do you watch? What is the general emotional quality of the people you spend time with?

What ever you feed your mind and senses, that builds up the quality and state of your consciousness. If you read or watch psychologically disturbing or emotionally charged media, your consciousness will become colored with that energetic pattern. If you spend time with angry, depressed or confused people, you will resonate in that pattern as well. You will have a harder time meditating than someone who gets their nourishment from long peaceful hikes in the sunshine, or who spends their time with quiet, purposeful and happy people, or who chooses to read spiritually uplifting and inspirational literature.

One thing you might want to ask yourself, is "Why do I enjoy these psychologically and emotionally charged forms of entertainment?" It could indicate a boredom or dissatisfaction with life. It could also indicate that you do not really value your Self enough to treat yourself to wholesome and happier forms of enjoyment. If this is the case, admit it. Then do what you need to make choices which are more supportive of your endeavors to "awaken". This may involve a bit of therapy, or just some motivated will power. Everyone is different, and you must find your own way in this regard.

#5 Are You Really Interested in Clearer States of Consciousness

This is a question I don't think gets asked enough. A lot of people proclaim to be interested in spiritual growth, but their idea of spiritual growth might be skewed. Many think that upon awakening, they will become super human. Magical powers will become evident in them. They will know everything. Suffering will never touch their life situation. This shows an interest in fantasy, not understanding.

If you are simply interested in relaxation and learning to be happier in general, keep meditating and smiling. But it takes more than a simple meditation relaxation practice to wake up. You need intention, drive, motivation and patience. You need to seek out people who can help you experience more clarity and spend time with them. You need to assess your life and make sure you are making choices that keep you from being unduly distracted during meditation, so you can focus your attention on deeper matters, beyond relaxation.

When you wake up in the morning, and when you sit to meditate, inwardly proclaim that you are here to wake up, and you are happy about it. Proclaim that you are looking forward to greater Self-knowledge and wisdom with each new day. Mean it! Accept it as true for you! Relax into that reality, as though it is as natural as the sun rising every morning.

Once we develop a consistent meditation practice, and it has served to de-stress our nervous system, and give us a measure of peace through withdrawing our often over stimulated senses, we have created an internal shelter. Now we can direct our attention to higher matters, such as exploring our true nature and our relationship with the divine.

Satisfying, Enjoyable, Exploration

Over time, meditation becomes enjoyable and deeply satisfying. Once we master the basics, and can set up the proper environment to meditate with ease, we find that all the hard work and practice pays off. This will be the case with any activity we want to excel at and master. Learning to water ski, playing poker well, enjoying successful business interactions, singing, etc; all of these require a lot of commitment to master the fundamentals. Yet, once mastered, a person can enjoy the activity with zeal.

For some reason many people think that just by saying they are on a spiritual path, they expect meditation to be knock-your-socks-off-fantastic. Realistically, it can be that way, but we need to be honest with ourselves, that it might take some time and training to get there. By now, we know what we need to do to make spiritual exploration and meditation as enjoyable as getting in a nice hot bath after a long day's work in the cold. (If you still aren't sure what you need to do, please review all past chapters up to this point.)

Enquiry is for really contemplating, discovering and feeling out what we are. Once we are settled, we must direct our attention to truly analyzing and contemplating our Self.
 -Nisgaradatta Maharaj

What Can You Do Now, to Make the Most of Your Practice, and Experience Spiritual Growth as the Masters Do?

#1 - Take some time to reflect on what you would like to know, spiritually speaking.

- Are you interested in experiencing a cosmic conscious state, beyond the ego and your personality and history?

- Do you want to have a greater sense of life and your relationship to the wholeness?

- Do you want to know what it is like to know God's infinite Love?

- Do you want to know beyond a doubt, that you are eternal and immortal?

These questions are very important. Once you have direct knowledge of the answers, a lot of doubt and despair in your life will evaporate. Get clear on what you really want to know.

Write it down. Write down why you want to know this? Once you have a clear definition of what you want to explore in your spiritual practice, state with intention that you are willing to do the work to have the realization. At the beginning of your meditations, state your intention again. Say, "I am doing my part to know the truth of my being." Then say, "And I allow the grace and compassion of the infinite to do what I cannot do."

That which was there in deep sleep (no I) there was happiness. Now we have an I and are asking to find happiness. Where there is I there is no happiness.
                                          -Nisgaradatta Maharaj

#2 - To experience a cosmic conscious state, beyond your personal history and limited knowledge as an individualized unit of the One Reality, you need to expand your boundaries. After you have meditated using a technique you've found useful, and are rather peaceful and settled, lift your awareness up into your crown chakra, or just hold your awareness about an inch or two above your head. With your awareness at this point, simultaneously focus on your breathing.

Now, as you do this, acknowledge who you think you are. Acknowledge the quirks of your personality, the failures you've made, the successes you've experienced, the people you surround your self with, how you feel like you belong to a certain family, how you define your self as having a particular career. With each breath release your attachment to one defining characteristic of your personality at a time. When you've run out of characteristics to release (This process may or may not take awhile. Time doesn't really matter, so don't rush it.) then continue with a relaxed yet attentive focus on the breath and the crown of your head.

With each breath feel yourself moving through the crown and expanding. Your boundaries are no longer confined to your skin. Imagine what it would feel like to be aware of the room around you, then the house, the city, the continent, world, solar system, galaxy, etc, until you reach the edges of the known universe. Go beyond that, then rest in that experience.

At first this may seem like simple imagination, and it will be. It may be hard to imagine your consciousness as encompassing the city, the galaxy, etc. Go as far as you can. As your imagination becomes engaged with each daily practice, you release your identification with your limited form. In time, your imagination will give way to the direct experience.

This practice will also work to encourage a greater sense of your connection to the wholeness of life.

#3 - To know what it is like to know the experience of God's Infinite Love, repeat the above procedure. This time, once you have expanded as far as your imagination and consciousness will allow at present, rest there.

Now as you breathe, remember a time when you felt perfectly cared for and loved, or imagine what that would feel like. On each breath, send that feeling out into your expanded awareness on the exhale. On the inhale, feel that same love, with intensity, rushing back through the cosmos and into your body.

No matter what arises in your mind during this practice, whether seemingly good or bad thoughts or distractions, let unconditional love flood the cosmos with each breath. If you have a hard time feeling love, you may have to practice feeling it. Use past memories to help access the feeling. The deeper your practice, the greater will be your ability to accept and feel what is always there, a deep abiding love and peacefulness, that is God's (and your) very being.

#4 - To know beyond a doubt that you are eternal and immortal, the above exercises are helpful, as they lift you out of your mistaken sense of self. Yet there is a special way to know your eternity and immortality.

As you sit in the silence after effectively practicing your meditation technique, then ask yourself, "What am I?" Sit quietly and wait for a response to come up for you, either as a thought, feeling, or sensation. Ask again. Continue to objectively watch what rises into your awareness with each asking. "What am I?"

After a while of practicing in this way, then ask your self, "What is it that is aware, of these things (that which has arisen in your awareness)?" Continue to reflect, asking this question.

You will find that on each asking, "What is aware of these changes in consciousness, that I think I am?" You will become aware that there is something that you cannot see, that is the witness, the observer. Get comfortable existing as that unconditioned, quiet, clear presence that sees and experiences all things.

Once you have this direct experience and can maintain it, you will know your immortal nature. You will know that this same presence, that you are, has been there when you were dreaming last night, when you were at your work two days ago, during your first day of school, and even before you were born. You will know your eternity.

These practices need to be performed on a regular basis until you have the direct experience of their fruition. This may take days, weeks, months, or even years. Yet, the knowledge provided by these realizations is superior to any other kind of knowledge.

Knowing what you are puts to rest most of your other burning questions, and releases you from much doubt and despair. Needless to say, if you are going to contemplate anything, contemplate what has been covered in this chapter. Then, get on with your immortal life.

ABOUT THE AUTHOR

Ryan Kurczak completed training with The American Institute of Vedic Studies and the European Institute of Vedic Studies in the subjects of Yoga, Ayurveda and Jyotish. He has studied astrology intensively under Richard Fish and Ernst Wilhelm.

Ryan was initiated into Kriya Yoga by a direct disciple of Paramahansa Yogananda. He teaches group meditation, Kriya Yoga practices, and the Yoga Sutras at various Yoga and New Thought Centers, and works with sincere students individually.

He lives in Asheville, NC where he works as a Vedic Astrologer, offering phone and internet astrological sessions.

See: www.AshevilleVedicAstrology.com.

Other Books By The Author

Kriya Yoga: Continuing the Lineage of Enlightenment

The Art and Science of Vedic Astrology:
The Foundation Course
(Co-Authored with Richard Fish)

The Art and Science of Vedic Astrology Vol. II:
Intermediate Techniques and Applied Chart Assessment
(Co-Authored with Richard Fish)
Available September 2013